ThinkBetter
LiveBetter

A Victorious Life Begins in Your Mind

Joel Osteen

Faith
Words

LARGE PRINT

ALSO BY JOEL OSTEEN

Break Out!
Break Out! Journal
Daily Readings from Break Out!
Every Day a Friday
Every Day a Friday Journal
Daily Readings from Every Day a Friday
Fresh Start
Fresh Start Study Guide
I Declare
I Declare Personal Application Guide
The Power of I Am
Daily Readings from The Power of I Am
The Power of I Am Journal
The Power of I Am Study Guide
Wake Up to Hope Devotional
You Can, You Will
You Can, You Will Journal
Daily Readings from You Can, You Will
Your Best Life Now
Daily Readings from Your Best Life Now
Your Best Life Begins Each Morning
Your Best Life Now Study Guide
Your Best Life Now for Moms
Your Best Life Now Journal
Starting Your Best Life Now

FaithWords
Hachette Book Group
1290 Avenue of the Americas
New York, NY 10104
faithwords.com
twitter.com/faithwords

First Edition: October 2016

FaithWords is a division of Hachette Book Group, Inc.
The FaithWords name and logo are trademarks of
Hachette Book Group, Inc.

The publisher is not responsible for websites (or their content) that are not owned by
the publisher.

The Hachette Speakers Bureau provides a wide range of authors for speaking events.
To find out more, go to www.hachettespeakersbureau.com or call (866) 376-6591.

Scriptures noted from *The Message*. Copyright © 1993, 1994,
1995, 1996, 2000, 2001, 2002. Used by permission of
NavPress Publishing Group.

Literary development: Lance Wubbels Literary Services,
Minneapolis, Minnesota.

Library of Congress Cataloging-in-Publication Data

Names: Osteen, Joel, author.
Title: Think better, live better : deleting negative thoughts, labels, and
    attitudes / Joel Osteen.
Description: First Edition. | New York : FaithWords, 2016.
Identifiers: LCCN 2016022264| ISBN 9780892969678 (hardcover) | ISBN
    9781455541706 (large print) | ISBN 9781609418250 (audio book) | ISBN
    9781478938965 (audio download) | ISBN 9780892969289 (ebook)
Subjects: LCSH: Thought and thinking—Religious aspects—Christianity. |
    Attitude (Psychology)—Religious aspects—Christianity.
Classification: LCC BV4598.4 .O88 2016 | DDC 248.4—dc23 LC record available at
https://lccn.loc.gov/2016022264

ISBNs: 978-0-8929-6967-8 (hardcover), 978-1-4789-4392-1
(B&N autographed hardcover), 978-1-4555-4170-6 (large print),
978-1-4555-9834-2 (international trade paperback),
978-0-8929-6928-9 (ebook), 978-1-4789-4531-4
(South African paperback)

Printed in the United States of America

RRD-C

10 9 8 7 6 5 4 3 2 1

CONTENTS

ThinkBetter
LiveBetter

CHAPTER ONE

Reprogram Your Mind

Our mind is like a computer. How we program it is the way it's going to function. You can have the most powerful computer ever made, the latest and fastest model, with the maximum amount of memory available, but if you put the wrong software in it, it's not going to function as it was designed. We've all had to deal with computer viruses. They can get into a perfectly good computer and start to contaminate the software. Before long the computer is slow, then you can't access your files. None of these problems occur because it's defective or poorly made. The computer's hardware is fine. It's because somebody reprogrammed the software. Somehow the insides got messed up. Now the software is contaminated.

In a similar way, when God created you, He stepped back and said, "Another masterpiece." Your hardware is perfect. You're the right size, the right nationality, and you have the right gifts. Not only that, God put the right software in you. From the very beginning, He programmed you to be victorious, healthy, strong, and creative. Your original software says, "You can do all things through Christ." He programmed, "Whatever you touch will prosper and succeed." He programmed, "You are the head and not the tail. You will lend and not borrow. You are a victor and not a victim." You were programmed to live an abundant, victorious, faith-filled life. That's how your Creator designed you.

The reason we don't always experience this abundant life is that we've allowed viruses to contaminate our software. We say to ourselves, "I'll never be successful. I'm not that talented." "I'll never break this addiction. I've had it

You were programmed to live an abundant, victorious, faith-filled life.

too long." "I'm slow, clumsy, and unattractive. Nothing good is in my future." Because our software is infected, we go around with low self-esteem, we're negative, we don't believe our dreams will come to pass, and we don't expect problems to turn around.

Here's the good news, though. There is nothing wrong with you. Like that computer, you're not a mistake. You're not defective or faulty. The problem is in your software. You have to get rid of the viruses. All through the day, dwell on what your Creator says about you. "I'm blessed. I'm strong. I'm healthy. I'm confident. I'm attractive. I'm valuable. I'm victorious." You have to get back to your original software. If your thinking is limited, your life will be limited. When you think better, you'll live better.

Learn to Hit the Delete Button

To restore our original software, one of the best things we can learn to do is hit the delete button. When negative, discouraging thoughts come trying to contaminate your software, just hit delete before they start affecting how you live. That thought says, *You've seen your best days. It's all downhill from here.* Recognize that's a virus trying to keep you from your destiny. It's real simple. Delete. Say to yourself, "I'm not dwelling on that. My software says, 'The path of the righteous gets brighter and brighter.'"

You'll never get well. You saw the medical report. Delete. Replace it by saying, "God is restoring health back to me. The number of my days He will fulfill."

You'll never accomplish your dreams. You're not that talented. You don't have what it takes. Delete. Delete. Delete. "I am fearfully and wonderfully made. I have the favor of God. Whatever I touch prospers and succeeds."

You'll never break that addiction. Your father was an alcoholic, and you'll be one, too. Delete. "No weapon formed against me will prosper. Whom the Son sets free is free indeed, and I am free."

If you're going to reach your highest potential, you have to get good at hitting the delete button.

> *If you're going to reach your highest potential, you have to get good at hitting the delete button.*

When I stepped up to pastor the church, every thought told me, *You can't do this, Joel. You don't know how to minister. You're too young. You don't have the experience. Nobody is going to come.* It would have been easy to let that virus take root and keep me from my destiny. I did what I'm asking you to do. I kept hitting the delete button. *You can't do it.* Delete. *You're too young.* Delete. *Nobody is going to come.* Delete. *You don't have the experience.* Delete. *It's not going to work out.* Delete. I wouldn't be where I am today if I hadn't become an expert at hitting the delete button.

Guard Your Mind

The Scripture tells us to guard our mind. You control the doorway to what you allow in. You can dwell on every negative thought and every derogatory comment, or you can choose to delete it and dwell on what God says about you. If I had let those negative thoughts play over and over in my mind, they would have contaminated my confidence, contaminated my self-esteem, and contaminated my future.

Why don't you start hitting the delete button? Quit dwelling on every negative thought that comes to your mind. That's the enemy trying to contaminate your software. If he can control your thinking, he can control your whole life. If the thought is negative, discouraging, pushing you down, don't dwell on it. Delete it. Pay attention to what you're thinking. If you go around thinking that you're not talented, you'll never have the confidence to step into your destiny. If you think you're unattractive, you'll never meet the people you were supposed to meet. If you think you can't break the addiction, you can't. If you think you've reached your limits, you have. It's not because you can't go further. You've just convinced yourself that you can't.

The good news is that it's not too late. You can still become everything God created you to be. Here's a key: You have to clear out all the negative things people have said about you. You are not who people say you are. You are who God says you are. Clear out the negative things that the coach or the teacher said about you. "You're too small. You don't have what it takes." Delete it. Quit dwelling on that. You're the right size. You have exactly what you need for the race that's been designed for you.

You have to clear out all the negative things people have said about you.

Clear out what the counselor said. "You're just a C student. You're not college material." Delete it. You're an A student. You have seeds of greatness.

Clear out what the ex-boyfriend or the ex-spouse said. "You're not attractive. You're not good enough for me." Delete it. You're a masterpiece, one of a kind, beautiful, attractive, a prized possession.

You may have to clear out what a parent said about you. "You're so undisciplined. You're never going to amount to much. You can't do anything right." Delete it. You are destined to do great things. You're destined to leave your mark on this generation.

Water the Right Seeds

I read a report about children who had been bullied in school. It talked about how, years later, those negative words from bullies were still having an effect on many of them. The researchers interviewed one man who was in his forties. He looked to be a bright, intelligent man, but he had not been able to hold down a good job, he struggled in his relationships, and he just couldn't seem to get his life on course. He told how as a child he was chubby, and some of the other children made fun of him and called him names such as "loser" and "failure." He made the mistake of letting those words take root in his thinking, and it had a dramatic impact on his life. It was keeping him in mediocrity.

When somebody calls you something, either good or bad, that seed is planted in your soil. Now you get to determine whether or not that seed takes root and grows. When you dwell on what was said, you are watering the seed. You're giving it a right to become a reality. That's why it's so important that we're disciplined in our thought life. It's great when people tell you, "You're blessed. You're talented. You're going to do great things." Water those seeds. Meditate on those throughout the day. That's what you want to become a reality.

But too often we make the mistake of watering the wrong seeds. If you allow negative things that other people say about you to take root, it's not their fault. They can't make a seed take root in you. All they can do is sow the seed. You have complete control over what seeds are going to grow in your own soil. A lot of times we blame others. "They were talking about me. They tried to make me look bad. They were criticizing me." Let them talk all they want. You control your own soil. Don't dwell on the negative. Don't replay what they said over and over. Guard your mind. Those are viruses trying to infiltrate your software.

This is what the Lord told Joshua after Moses had died and he was to lead the Israelites into the Promised Land: "If you will meditate on what God says about you day and night, you will have good success and prosper in everything you do." When your mind is filled with thoughts of faith, thoughts of hope, and thoughts of victory, that's what will become a reality.

Do you know why that man who was in his forties was still struggling? He let those derogatory comments play over and over in his mind. Every time he thought about it, he was watering that seed year after year. It's sad to say, but it became a reality. How different would his life be if he had just learned to hit the delete button? Instead of constantly playing the negative, he should have gone around thinking, *I'm a masterpiece. I'm one of a kind. I'm talented. I've got seeds of greatness.* It would have been a whole different story.

Reprogram Your Software

Are there any viruses that are contaminating your computer? Are you allowing what people have spoken over you to hold you back? We can't stop the negative voices from speaking, but we can choose whether or not we're going to dwell on what they say. God has given each of us a delete button.

I talked with a man who was raised by a very negative father. His father was always putting him down, telling him what he couldn't become. Not surprisingly, this son, when he was in his twenties and even through his thirties, couldn't seem to ever get ahead. Life was always a struggle. He had a college degree, but he couldn't get a good job and couldn't keep a steady relationship. He told how his father's words were always playing in the back of his mind: "You'll never be successful. You don't have what it takes." Even when his father was on his deathbed, he looked at him and said, "Your brother never amounted to anything, and you won't either." Those were the last words he ever heard his father speak. For years he went around with a smoldering anger, feeling inferior, and all of that negativity acted like an anchor on his life. He wouldn't take a new position. He didn't feel qualified. He was too afraid. All these bondages were the result of the words that were spoken over him. We know the importance of a father's blessing, what weight that carries, but unfortunately some people don't receive that blessing.

One day this man heard me talking about wrong mind-sets and making sure you don't have things that are holding you back. He realized that his father's words had become a stronghold in his mind. He started hitting the delete button, reprogramming his software. When he heard, "You don't have what it takes," he hit delete and said, "I'm equipped. I'm empowered. I'm well able." When he heard, "You'll never amount to anything," he hit delete and declared, "I will fulfill my destiny. I will become all that God has created me to be."

Today this gentleman is extremely successful and has a beautiful family. They volunteer at our services. Everything changed when he started hitting the delete button. Maybe you are like him and you didn't receive your earthly father's blessing. The good news is that you have your Heavenly Father's blessing. Almighty God is saying to you, "You are My masterpiece. You are one of a kind. You have seeds of greatness. You are equipped, strong, talented, and beautiful." That's what should be playing in your mind. No matter who tried to tell you otherwise—a parent, a friend, a coach, a neighbor—delete that and reprogram your software. You are not defective. You are not flawed. You have been fearfully and wonderfully made.

> *You are not defective. You are not flawed. You have been fearfully and wonderfully made.*

You may have been through unfair situations. People have spoken things over you that they had no business saying. You could easily go around feeling bad, having low self-esteem, low self-worth. But don't ever let what someone said or what someone did keep you from knowing who you really are. You are a child of the Most High God. You have royal blood flowing through your veins. God has crowned you with His favor. People may have tried to push you down and make you feel insignificant, but that does not change who you are. You are still the apple of God's eye. You are still His most prized possession. God still has an amazing future in front of you. If you will hit that delete button and get rid of any strongholds, God will take what was meant for your harm and He will use it to your advantage. The psalmist said, "Even if my father and mother forsake me, God will adopt me as His very own child."

The Battle Takes Place in Your Mind

I know a lady who struggled with her self-worth for many years. Growing up, she never felt she was good enough or that she fit in. These insecurities stemmed from being a child born out of wedlock. Her mother and father weren't married. One day, as a little girl, she saw her birth certificate and noticed the box was checked that said, "Illegitimate." That phrase became ingrained in her thinking. All through her childhood and her teenage years, anytime she tried to move forward, these words would come up in her mind once again. "You're a mistake. Nobody even wanted you. You're not valuable." She believed the lies, which dramatically affected her personality, her attitude, and even her marriage.

One day she discovered that our worth and value doesn't come from people; it comes from Almighty God. She said, "It was like something exploded on the inside." She decided to start hitting the delete button. When thoughts came saying, *You're not valuable. You have no future*, instead of dwelling on them and letting them depress her, she reprogrammed her software. "I'm not a mistake. I'm not an accident. God chose me to be here before the foundation of the world. I'm accepted. I'm approved. I'm valuable." Her attitude was, *No matter what my birth certificate says, I know I am legitimate. Almighty God breathed His life into me.* Today, now that her thinking is better, she is living a blessed, free, confident life.

Make sure there are no strongholds in your mind that are keeping you back. I've learned that anytime we try to move forward in faith, there will always be people trying to contaminate our software. They may not do it on purpose, but they'll tell you what you can't do and why it's not going to work out. "My cousin tried and failed." "My grand-mother died of that same disease." The negative voices will come out of the woodwork. But remember, God didn't put the promise in them. God put the promise in you. Don't let people talk you out of your destiny.

That's why we start off every message by saying, "I am who God says I am." We're saying in effect, "I am not who my history teacher says I am. I am not who my ex-spouse says I am. I am not who the critics say I am. I am who God says I am." I like to take it one step further. "Not only am I who God says I am, but I can do what God says I can do." That means we know we've been programmed for victory. We've been programmed to reign in life. We've been programmed to overcome obstacles. We will accomplish our dreams. We will meet the right people. We will step into the fullness of our destiny. When you think like that, all the forces of darkness cannot stop you.

The real battle is taking place in your mind. If you're defeated in your thoughts, you've already lost. You have to get rid of the viruses if you want to live better. If you will get back to the original software that was installed in you by your Creator, you'll go places that you've never dreamed.

Consider How You Were Programmed

It's interesting how little children start off so excited about life. They have big dreams. They're going to become a scientist, an astronaut, a singer, a teacher, a ballplayer, even the president. They're not intimidated. They're not insecure. They believe they can do anything. It's because they just came from their Creator. Their thinking has not been contaminated. They can still feel the seeds of greatness. But over time, too often they start to get reprogrammed. Somebody tells them what they *can't* become, what they *can't* do. Little by little their environment starts to squeeze down on them. A coach says, "You're not good enough. You're too small." Their self-esteem goes down. They see somebody more attractive, who is getting all sorts of attention, and they start to feel inferior. All these things begin to distort their thinking about who they really are. Before long, instead of dreaming big and believing possibility thoughts, they think, *I'll never do anything great. I'm not that talented. I'm just average.*

When we find ourselves stuck in these ruts, not believing we can rise any higher, we need to ask, "Why do I think this way? Who programmed me to think that I'm average? Who programmed me to give up on my dreams? Who programmed me to think I can't lose this weight, I can't break this addiction, I've gone as far as I can? Where did those thoughts come from?" Could it be that you have accepted a wrong mind-set because of the environment you were raised in, from the people you were around? Just because it seems normal to you doesn't necessarily mean that it *is* normal.

Could it be that you have accepted a wrong mind-set because of the environment you were raised in?

Sometimes we've just learned to function in our dysfunction. Maybe everybody you grew up with was negative, but you're not supposed to be negative. Negative is not normal thinking. Maybe your friends didn't have big dreams. They didn't do anything great in life, but that's not okay for you. That's not normal. Just because family members had addictions and bad habits, don't make the mistake of thinking that it's okay for you to live that way. Those are viruses that have been passed down, that keep infiltrating your thinking and affecting your living. God created you to go further, to live confidently, to be free, to be healthy, positive, and happy. You have greatness on the inside. Get it started by reprogramming your thinking.

I heard a story about a German shepherd that was pregnant with puppies. One day she was walking across the street and got hit by a car. Both her back legs were broken, but she was able to drag herself off the street and back to her house. As the weeks went by, she slowly recovered. Her legs finally healed, but because they weren't properly reset, all she could do was drag her back legs. She couldn't walk properly. Her joints had been messed up. Eventually she had her puppies. They seemed healthy and whole, but several weeks later, when they started walking, they dragged their back legs just like their mother did. The owner was amazed. He thought maybe they had been injured in the accident as well. He took them to the veterinarian to have them checked out. The doctor discovered there was nothing wrong with their back legs. They were perfectly healthy. The puppies were simply copying their mother. That's all they had seen modeled. In their minds, that was the way they were supposed to walk.

That's what has happened to many of us—we copied what we saw modeled growing up. The people who raised us were good people. They were doing their best, but in some ways they were dragging their back legs. They were negative, discouraged. Now we live negative, discouraged. They had addictions and low self-esteem. Now we struggle in those same areas. Maybe they made poor choices in relationships and became involved with the wrong people. Now we're dealing with the same issues. We saw them accept mediocrity. Mediocrity has become normal to us.

The good news is, just like with those puppies, there is nothing wrong with your back legs. Those are simply wrong mind-sets you've developed. As you get your thinking straightened out, your legs will straighten out. God didn't make you faulty. He didn't create you subpar. He created you in His image. You are His masterpiece, crowned with favor, equipped with talent and gifts. You are destined to live a healthy, abundant, happy, faith-filled life. Don't go around dragging your back legs. You are not supposed to go through life feeling inferior, held down by low self-esteem, addicted, having small goals and small dreams. That's not who you are. Start reprogramming your mind as the head and not the tail. Program it with excellence, not mediocrity. Program it with abundance, not lack and poverty. Program it with freedom, not addictions.

Strongholds Are Coming Down

This is what my father did. He grew up in a very poor environment. His parents lost everything during the Great Depression. He had no money, a poor education, and no future to speak of. He had been programmed with poverty, defeat, and mediocrity. That's all he had ever seen. He could have settled and lived there, thinking, *This is my lot in life. We're just poor defeated people.* But at seventeen years old, when he gave his life to Christ, he started reprogramming his thinking. Deep down, something said, "You were made for more than this. You're not supposed to constantly struggle, to barely make it through life." He could feel those seeds of greatness stirring on the inside. His attitude was, *This may be where I am, but this is not who I am. I may be in defeat, but I am not defeated. I'm a child of the Most High God.*

Day after day, he kept hitting the delete button. A thought told him, *You have no future.* Delete. "God's plans for me are for good, to give me a future and a hope."

You have no money. Delete. "I'm blessed. Whatever I touch prospers."

You didn't even finish school. You'll never get out of here. It's impossible. Delete. Delete. Delete. "God is making a way where I don't see a way. He is opening doors that no man can shut. He is bringing the right people across my path. I will step into the fullness of my destiny."

He reprogrammed his thinking with thoughts of faith, thoughts of hope, and thoughts of victory. As his thinking improved, he rose up out of that poverty and set a new standard for our family.

You may have been raised in a limited environment. All you saw modeled was strife, addictions, conflict, low self-esteem, and mediocrity. Don't let that set the limits for your life. Don't go around dragging your back legs. God wants you to go further. It starts by getting rid of viruses. Hit the delete button. A thought tells you, *You've gone as far as you can.* Delete. *You'll never get well.* Delete. *You'll always be addicted.* Delete. *This is as good as it gets.* Delete.

If you will get good at hitting the delete button, you will break out of bondages and step into freedom. You will break out of lack and poverty and step into abundance. You will break out of mediocrity and step up to excellence. This is a new day. Strongholds are coming down. Wrong mind-sets are being broken. Viruses are being cleared out. Get ready for God to do something new. Get ready to see His goodness in amazing ways.

Clear Out Every Virus

When Carl Lewis was training for the Olympic Games, the experts said no person can jump over thirty feet. Scientists had run their calculations, done all their research. According to their data, no one could ever jump that far. A reporter asked Carl Lewis what he thought about it. He responded, "Yes, I know the experts say it can't be done, but I don't listen to that kind of talk. Thoughts like that have a way of sinking into your feet." He went on later that same year to jump over thirty feet and break the world record.

Are you allowing negative thoughts to sink into your feet, to stifle your potential, to handicap your life's race? Why don't you do what he did? Start hitting the delete button. God has the final say. He wouldn't have put the dream in your heart or given you that promise if He didn't have a way to bring it to pass.

Delete what the naysayers have told you.

Delete the discouraging words. Delete the negative reports. You have to get back to your original software. Who told

Are you allowing negative thoughts to sink into your feet, to stifle your potential?

you that you can't be successful? Who told you that you can only make Cs in school? Who told you you're not tall enough, not smart enough, that you've reached your limits? I can assure you those words did not come from your Creator. Those are viruses trying to contaminate your software. Don't let what anyone told you or what anyone modeled for you limit your life. There is nothing wrong with your back legs. Start reprogramming your mind. All through the day, dwell on what your Creator says about you. "I'm blessed. I'm healthy. I'm talented. I'm valuable. My best days are still out in front of me."

If you'll do this, I believe and declare, every virus is being cleared out, even right now. Strongholds are coming down. Wrong mind-sets that have held you back for years will no longer have any effect on you. As Joshua was promised, you will have good success and prosper in everything you do.

CHAPTER TWO

Remove Negative Labels

As a teenager, Walt Disney was told by a newspaper editor that he wasn't creative, that he didn't have a good imagination. Lucille Ball was told that she didn't have any acting skills, that she should try a different profession. Winston Churchill was not thought of as a good student and twice failed the entrance examination into the Royal Military College Sandhurst. The common denominator in the success of these people is that they chose to remove the negative labels. Because they thought better than what others said, they lived far better than the labels had read.

It's the same way today. People are constantly

putting labels on us, telling us what we can and cannot become, what we do or don't have. Many times, these labels are not in agreement with what God says about us; but if we don't know any better, we'll wear them like they're the truth. The sad thing is that if we keep them on long enough, they'll become so ingrained in our thinking we'll become what people have said rather than what God has said.

I met a gentleman who was told by his high school counselor that he was not that talented and he should focus on the lowest-skilled job he could find. That counselor stuck a label on him—"below average, barely getting by, not talented." He wore that label year after year, thinking, *I'm not that smart. I just don't have what it takes.* After high school, he got a job at a local factory and stayed at the lowest level for years,

> *People are constantly putting labels on us, telling us what we can and cannot become.*

just as he'd been told. One day the factory closed, so he went across town and applied at another factory. This company had a policy that every applicant had to take an IQ test. He took the test and his IQ score was assessed at the genius level. The owner called him in and said, "What are you doing applying for this low-level position? You scored the highest of anyone in our company's sixty-three-year history." That day a stronghold was broken in this man's mind. He removed a label that had held him back for seventeen years. He eventually started his own company and went on to invent several products that are now patented and in the marketplace.

As this man did, if you're going to rise to the next level, you have to remove any negative labels that are holding you back. To live better, you need to think better. Has someone convinced you that you've reached your limit and gone as far as you can go? Or that you've made too many mistakes? "You're all washed up." "You'll never accomplish your dreams."

"You don't have the resources." Don't go through life wearing any of those labels.

People don't determine our destiny; God does.

Labels Are Like Weeds

When my father went to be with the Lord in 1999, I stepped up to pastor the church. I had never ministered before. One Sunday, after the service, I overheard two ladies talking in the lobby. One said, "Joel's not as good as his father."

The other answered back, "Yes, I don't think the church is going to last."

I was already insecure. I already felt unqualified, and *boom*, another negative label was stuck on me. "Not good enough. Not up to par. Inferior." That's the way the enemy works. He would love to put labels on you to limit your thinking and keep you from reaching your highest potential. He doesn't fight you for where you are. He fights you for where you're going. He knows God has amazing things in your future, so he will try to discourage you, intimidate you, and make you feel inferior.

Words are like seeds. If you dwell on them long enough, they will take root and you will become what was said.

I tried to remove that negative label, but it wasn't easy. Those thoughts played in my mind again and again. "You don't have what it takes. You're not as good as your father." It was like trying to peel off a bumper sticker that has been on a car for a long time. You peel it, and it tears. You have to keep working and working. I fought those thoughts day after day. Finally, I removed that negative label, and I put on a new label: "I can do all things through Christ. I am strong in the Lord. I am anointed."

If I had made the mistake of wearing that negative label, I don't believe I would be where I am today. Wrong labels can keep you from your destiny. Don't go the next twenty years allowing negative comments to hold you back. You are not who people say you are. You are who God says you are. People will label you "not good enough, too slow, too old, too many mistakes." God labels you "strong, talented, valuable, more than a conqueror." Those are the thoughts that will help you to live better.

Are there labels holding you back today? What a coach said? What a counselor said? Even negative comments spoken by your parents? The only power that a label has over you is the power that you give it. If you remove it, quit thinking about it, quit acting like it's the truth, then that label will have no effect on you.

> *The only power that a label has over you is the power that you give it.*

Those two ladies said the church wouldn't last and that I didn't have the talent. But they couldn't stop my destiny. They couldn't stop what God had already ordained. The only way they could have limited me is if I had worn their negative label around.

The Real Battle Takes Place in Your Mind

A man told me how he overheard his junior high teacher telling his mother that he was a slow learner. For thirty years he wore that label around and never had a good job, never had any real success. He just floundered through life under the weight of that negative thought. One day I told him what I'm telling you. "You have to remove that label. Your teacher may have been sincere. She may have made an assessment based on where you were at the time, but she didn't know what God put in you. If you're going to become who you were created to be, you have to say, 'No, thanks. I am not wearing that "slow learner" label anymore. That may have been her opinion, but I have another opinion. It's from my Creator, and He says that I have the mind of Christ, I am full of wisdom, and I can fulfill my destiny.'"

Don't let negative labels hold you back.

I talked to a high school student one time. She was about to take her final exams. She asked, "Joel, will you pray that God will help me to make Cs on these tests?"

"Why do we want to pray for Cs and not As?" I responded.

"Oh no, Joel!" she exclaimed. "My high school counselor told me I'm just a C student."

She didn't know any better. Somebody stuck a label on her. She was wearing it around like it was the truth.

Have you ever thought that the same God who can help you make a C can help you make an A? Why don't you remove that label? The same God who can help you get by in life can help you excel in life. The same God who can give you an apartment can give you a beautiful house.

Do you need to remove any labels? The label, "divorced"—*I'll never meet anyone new.* The label, "overweight"—*I'll never get in shape.* The label, "addicted"—*I'll never break these bad habits.* Whatever label you're wearing, you're going to become what that label says. You're giving that thought the power to shape and control how you live.

This is why some people can't break an addiction. They're wearing the label, "addict." The real battle is taking place

> *Whatever label you're wearing, you're going to become what that label says.*

in your mind. If you think you're an addict, you will live as an addict. You have to change the label. God says you are free. You are clean. You are healthy. You are whole. Don't go the next twenty years wearing the "addict" label. Put on some new labels today.

Remove Any Label That Is Holding You Back

A young man told me he was the main drug dealer in his neighborhood. He was sincere. He wasn't proud of it. He said matter-of-factly,

"Joel, I know this is not right. I don't like doing it, but it's the only thing that I'm good at." He was wearing that "drug dealer" label. It's all he thought he could do.

I told him, "If you can sell drugs, you can sell medical supplies. If you can sell drugs, you can sell stocks and bonds. Think about this. To sell drugs you have to get the word out. That's advertising. You have to manage your inventory. That's administration. You have to take care of your clients. That's customer service. Don't sell yourself short. Remove any labels that are holding you back."

Let me ask you who told you that all you can do is sell drugs. Some guy on a street corner? It's not the truth. Who told you that all you can make in school are Cs and not As? A counselor? They didn't know what God put in you. Who told you that you could never succeed, and that you'll not be as good as your father? Two ladies in the lobby? They can't determine your destiny. Who told you that you'll never own a nice house, that you'll never get married, that you'll never accomplish your dreams? Those labels did not come from your Creator.

Just because somebody spoke those labels over you doesn't mean they are the truth. You have the power to remove those negative labels. You've been wearing them way too long. Take off the label that says, "You'll never go to college; nobody in your family has." You can be the first. "You'll never get out of that neighborhood; all the odds are against you." That's what they told my father. He removed the label. He changed his thinking and totally changed his life. God took him places he never dreamed of going. "You'll never get well; that sickness is terminal." That's what they told my mother. She removed the label. Thirty-five years later, she is still healthy, whole, and strong.

You serve a supernatural God. He can do what medicine cannot do. He is not limited by your education, your background, or the family you come from. He's not shaken by the things people have spoken over you. He's not up in Heaven frantically trying to figure out how to get you to your destiny. He knows the end from the beginning. He already has solutions to problems you've not even had yet. He is all-powerful and all-knowing.

People may have tried to push you down with labels, but if you just remove those labels and get in agreement with God, He will lift you up. He will take you where you could not go on your own. You don't have to figure it all out. All God asks of you is to believe. When you believe, all things are possible. When you believe, doors will open that may never have opened otherwise. When you believe better, God will take you from the back to the front. Don't let negative labels hold you down.

People will tell you, "You're all washed up. You've made too many mistakes." If you wear that label, it will keep you from the amazing future God has in store for you. God says, "My mercy is bigger than any mistake." God says, "I will still get you to your destiny." God says, "I will give you beauty for ashes. I'll pay you back double for the unfair things that have happened." You wouldn't be alive unless God had another victory in your future. Why don't you take off the "washed-up" label. Take off the "failure," "guilty," "condemned" labels and put on these new labels: "redeemed," "restored," "forgiven," "bright future," "new beginning."

You Have an Amazing Future

There was a young lady in the Scripture named Rahab. She was a prostitute. She had made a lot of poor choices in life. I'm sure many people had written her off and considered her a scourge on society. No doubt she wore the labels "failure, outcast, not valuable, no future." It's easy to think that God surely wouldn't have any different labels for her to wear; she had made too many mistakes. But God never gives up on us.

One day Joshua and the Israelites were about to attack the city of Jericho, which is where Rahab lived. Joshua sent two men in to spy out the land. Word got to the king that spies had entered the city. Now they were in great danger. Of all the people whom God could have used to protect His people, He chose Rahab. Risking her own life, Rahab took the men into her home and hid them. When security forces came searching for the spies, she covered for them and told the king's men they had left the city before dark and could be caught if pursued quickly.

The two spies said to Rahab, "We're going to wipe out the whole city, but because you honored God by showing us favor, we will spare you and anyone in this home." When the city of Jericho was conquered, Rahab and her family were the only ones saved. What's interesting is that Rahab went on to marry a Jewish man named Salmon, and they had a son named Boaz. Boaz married Ruth, and they had a son named Obed. Obed married and had a son named Jesse. Jesse married and had a son named David. This means that Rahab, a former prostitute, is in the family line of Jesus Christ.

What am I saying? You are not what people label you. You are what God labels you. People labeled Rahab as "outcast, failure, not usable." God labeled her as "chosen, restored, valuable, a masterpiece." When that got into her thinking, everything about her life changed for the better. You may have made mistakes, but you need to remove the wrong labels. Quit thinking about what people have said about you. "He'll never amount to much. He's just too far out." "She'll never have a position of influence. I know what she used to do." "He'll never accomplish his dreams. He comes from the wrong family." Don't believe these lies. God has amazing things planned for your future.

You may be wearing the same labels that were stuck on Rahab—"too far out, too far gone, not religious enough." God loves to take people just like you and pour out His mercy and favor in ways you've never imagined. But it all starts with your thinking. You have to remove the negative labels. Quit telling yourself, "I'm washed up. I've made too many mistakes. I'm not talented. I'm not attractive." Put on this new label: "I'm restored, redeemed, anointed, equipped, and empowered."

People will tell you, "You're too small." "You're too quiet." "You don't have a good personality." "You come from the wrong family." Don't you dare go through life wearing these labels. You have been made in the image of Almighty God. God did not make any mistakes. You are the perfect size. You have the right personality, the right gifts, the right looks, and the right skin color. It says in Psalms that you have been "fearfully and wonderfully made." You are not an accident. God designed you precisely for the race He laid out for you. Remove the "too big," "too short," and "unattractive" labels. Put on this new label: "Fearfully and wonderfully made."

> *You have the right personality, the right gifts, the right looks, and the right skin color.*

You Are a Masterpiece

When I was growing up, I was very small. I grew six inches *after* high school. When I played basketball, at one point I was practically a foot shorter than my teammates. Somehow I got the nickname "Peanut." Everywhere I went, that's all I heard. "Hey, Peanut!" "Good morning, Peanut." During basketball games, in front of the whole high school, I heard, "Go, Peanut! Go!" The cheerleaders even had a cheer: "Big G. Little O. Go! Go!" I was the little O. Nobody said it derogatorily. They just said it in fun. But I must admit it didn't help my self-esteem. Every time I heard it, I was reminded of what I was not. "I'm not as tall as everybody else. I'm below average. I'm not up to par." I let that label stick, and I became less and less outgoing, quieter, more reserved, all because of a label that I allowed other people to put on me.

One day I did what I'm asking you to do.

I pulled off that label. I realized that when God made me, He didn't make a mistake. He made me just as I am on purpose. I may be small, but I know dynamite comes in small packages. In the same way, you are not too tall, too short, too old, or too young. God says you are a masterpiece. Now put your shoulders back, hold your head high, and wear this label proudly: "Child of the Most High God."

Today in our schools there is a lot of bullying. A parent told me how her ten-year-old son was being teased because he is a very eager learner. He's always reading books and taking extra classes. Even during recess, when the other kids are out playing, he'll go over to a table and work on his math. The other children would constantly give him a hard time and call him different names. But if you work hard, study hard, make good grades, and stay on the high road, you should not worry when people call you a "nerd," "geek," or "bookworm." Why? Because in a few years they'll call you "Boss." They won't be talking about you; they'll be working for you. Don't let their label keep you from becoming all that God created you to be.

One label that far too many people wear is the label "average." They say, "I'm just ordinary." I've had people tell me, "Joel, there's nothing special about me. I'm just one of the six billion people on the earth."

You were never created to live an average life. You have seeds of greatness on the inside. You were created to be a history maker. You're not supposed to live and die with nobody even knowing you were here. You were created to leave your mark on this generation. God has an assignment for you that nobody else can fulfill. God needs you. He needs your gifts, your smile, your love, your passion. You are a part of His divine plan. You have something to offer that nobody else can offer. Nobody else has your exact personality, your exact looks. There is something unique about you. Don't wear the "average" label. If you think you're average, you'll be average. If you think you're ordinary, you'll live an ordinary, get-by life and never do anything great.

The truth is, there is nothing ordinary about you. You have the fingerprints of God all over you. The Creator of the universe breathed His life into you. He crowned you with His favor. You have royal blood flowing through your veins. You have a destiny to fulfill, something greater than you've ever imagined. But if it's going to happen, if you're going to become all God has created you to be, one of the first things you will have to do is remove the "average" label, peel off the "ordinary" label. Put on these new labels: "masterpiece," "valuable," "one of a kind."

> *You were never created to live an average life. You have seeds of greatness on the inside.*

Giant Killer

When the prophet Samuel came to anoint one of Jesse's sons to be the next king of Israel, Jesse didn't even bother to bring his youngest son, David, in from the fields where he was taking care of the sheep. Jesse thought, *I know it's not David. He's too small, too young, not very talented, and not as smart as his brothers.* David had all these negative labels put on him by his own father.

When Samuel saw Eliab, David's oldest brother, he was very impressed with his outward appearance, but the Lord said, "It's not him." Six more sons of Jesse passed by, and Samuel said, "Not this one. Not this one. Not this one." Samuel finally came to the end of the line and then asked Jesse, "Do you have any other sons? It's none of these."

"Yes," Jesse answered, shaking his head. "My youngest son, David, is out in the shepherds' fields, but I know it's not him."

God doesn't label people the way people do. People usually look on the outside, but God looks on the heart. God knows what you are capable of. God can see the seeds of greatness He has placed in you. It's so easy to let what someone has spoken over us keep us from really believing in ourselves.

David walked in. Samuel took one look at him and said, "He's the one. That's the next king of Israel." Right then and there, David had to make the decision that I'm asking you to make. He had to peel off the negative labels. He had heard them a thousand times: "too young, too small, doesn't have what it takes."

What's interesting is that David's brothers, even though they saw Samuel anoint David as the next king, still tried to stick their negative labels on him. Later, when David left the shepherds' fields to visit his brothers out where the army had gathered to fight the Philistines, his oldest brother, Eliab, said, "David, what are you doing out here, and with whom have you left those few sheep you're supposed to be taking care of?" What was Eliab doing? Sticking a label on him: "inferior, not good enough, irresponsible, intimidated."

David could have said, "Yeah, you're right. What was I thinking? I should get back to the sheep." David could have accepted those old labels and let them hold him back, but this time David had a different attitude. He said, "Eliab, what you say about me doesn't change what God said about me. You're still labeling me 'weak, defeated, and inferior.' You don't realize that I've gotten rid of those labels, and the Creator of the universe, the God who breathed life into me, placed new labels on me: 'giant killer, more than a conqueror, destined for greatness, king of Israel.'"

You may have had negative things spoken over you, even by people who should have been encouraging you. I love what Isaiah said: "No weapon formed against you will ever prosper, but every tongue raised in judgment"—that means every negative label—"you will show to be in the wrong." Notice, God is not going to do it. *You* have to show it to be in the wrong. In other words, you have to remove the negative label. Nothing that was spoken over you has to define you, even if it was from people who raised you or grew up in the same home with you. Nothing that's happened in your past has to keep you from your destiny. Even if you've made mistakes or gone through unfair situations, you can show the negative things to be in the wrong by shaking off the self-pity and moving forward with your life.

Will you dare to do what David did and remove the negative labels? Quit dwelling on what your mama said, what a jealous sister said,

Nothing that was spoken over you has to define you.

what a cranky coworker said, or what a cynical neighbor said. You are not who people say you are. You are who God says you are. They cannot stop your destiny. Remove the old labels. I'll give you new labels to wear: "giant killer," "history maker," "world changer."

The Promise Is in You

My friend Dale Brown, the legendary coach of the LSU basketball team, told me about the time he was speaking to a group of soldiers at a military base in California. When he finished, a young man came up to him who stood nearly seven feet tall and weighed 250 pounds.

"Coach Brown," the young man said, "I want to try out for our basketball team, but I can't dunk the basketball. I can barely jump. When I run up and down the court, my legs tire out so quickly that I can only play a few minutes."

"How long have you been in the military, son?" Coach Brown asked him, gazing up at him, then down at his size-seventeen shoes.

"I'm not in the military, Coach. My father is. I'm thirteen years old."

Coach Brown immediately decided to take this young man under his wing. He said, "When I get back to Louisiana, I'm going to send you my training program. It will help strengthen your legs and increase your endurance."

Three months later, he got a letter from the young man saying, "Coach Brown, I've done everything you've asked me to do, spent hours in the gym and in the weight room working out. But my basketball coach just cut me from the team. He told me that I'm too big, too slow, too clumsy, that I'll never be able to play basketball." Nothing but negative labels were stuck to him.

Coach Brown wrote him back and said in effect, "Son, if you'll just keep working out, keep being your best each day, and keep asking God to help you, He will get you to where you're supposed to be."

That young man had to make a decision. "Am I going to wear these negative labels throughout my life? 'Too big.' 'Too slow.' 'Too clumsy.' Or am I going to follow the dream that God has placed in my heart? Am I going to think better and live better? Am I going to believe I'm a giant killer and I can do all things through Christ?" He decided to remove the negative labels.

That young man, Shaquille O'Neal, ended up going to LSU and playing college basketball for Coach Brown, where he broke all the records and became one of the greatest basketball players who ever played the game. Today there is a bronze statue of Shaquille—the clumsy kid who could barely jump—dunking the basketball in front of the LSU Tigers basketball practice facility. I wonder where he would be now if he had believed the negative labels, if he had thought, *My coach is right. I guess I am too big, too slow, too clumsy.* We wouldn't be talking about his nineteen-year NBA career today.

Has somebody told you that you can't accomplish your dreams? Like the two ladies in the lobby who said, "He's not talented. He's not like his father. He doesn't have the experience." God didn't put the promise in them. He put the promise in me. Along the way, there will always be negative voices trying to label you, but God would not have given you the dream unless He had already equipped you to fulfill it. You already have what you need. What may seem like a limitation today—too tall, too short—God can use as an asset. God knows what He is doing. He has designed you specifically for the race that you're in.

You may feel, like Shaquille, that you've been cut from the team. The experts have told you what you can't do, what you don't have. Here's what I've learned. The experts can be wrong. Experts built the *Titanic*, and it sank. Amateurs built the Ark, and it floated.

> *Experts built the* Titanic, *and it sank. Amateurs built the Ark, and it floated.*

The experts said that we would never have our facility, the former Compaq Center, but it's our home. The experts said that my father would never get out of poverty, but he did. The experts said that my mother wouldn't be alive today, but she is. The experts said that David was too small, but God said he was just the right size. The experts said that I couldn't pastor a large church, that I didn't have the experience, but they were wrong.

You Have a New Name

In the Scripture, a lady named Rachel died while giving birth to her second son. There were difficulties and complications in the labor and delivery, so much pain and agony. Right before she died as she was giving birth, she named the boy Ben-oni, which means "son of my sorrow." She labeled him based on what she had experienced. Now this little boy was going to go through life being called "son of my sorrow."

Sometimes people will put a negative label on you, not because of anything you've done, but because of the pain and heartache they've experienced. Hurting people end up hurting other people. Bitter people are quick to stick negative labels on other people.

A few minutes after Rachel died, her husband, Jacob, came rushing in. The nurse was holding the baby and handed him to Jacob, saying, "This is your son, Ben-oni, son of my sorrow."

When Jacob heard that, something came over him. He rose up and said, "No, that is not his name. No matter what he's been through in the past, my son will not be called 'son of sorrow.' His name will be Benjamin, which means 'son of strength, son of power, son of my right hand.'"

Benjamin grew up to become a great leader. Out of his family lineage came the kings of Israel, one king after another. God had a great destiny for Benjamin to fulfill, and He knew that if he went through life wearing that label, "son of my sorrow," he could never become what he was created to be. God stepped in and said, "No, no. He's not wearing that label. He's not a son of sorrow, not a son of defeat, not a son of disappointment. Benjamin is a son of destiny. This child has seeds of greatness. His name will be Son of Strength." God knows how powerful labels are.

Maybe somebody has tried to label you average, slow learner, not talented, too many mistakes. God is saying the same thing to you that He said to little Benjamin: "I am changing your name. I'm placing a new label on you. No more Son of Sorrow. No more Daughter of Mediocrity. No more Son of Broken Dreams. I'm renaming you Son of Strength, Daughter of Destiny, Child of Influence, Child of Greatness, Child of Victory." So remove the old labels and start going by your new names: Masterpiece, Valuable, One of a Kind, More Than a Conqueror, History Maker. These are the labels we are to be wearing.

I've learned that people can call you many different things, but you are not what people call you. You are what you answer to. They can call you slow, lazy, too old, all washed up. That's all right. Just don't answer to it. Answer to "victorious." Answer to "talented." Answer to "history maker." If you'll do this, I believe and declare, today is going to be a turning point. The bondages from the past are no longer going to have any effect on you. As you think better, you are going to rise up and become the son of strength, the daughter of influence, the child of victory, the child of blessing, the child of favor, the child of greatness. You will overcome every obstacle, defeat every enemy, and become everything God created you to be.

CHAPTER THREE

Release the Full You

Inside each of us is a blessed, prosperous, victorious person. This person is free from addictions and bad habits. This person is confident and secure, talented and creative, disciplined and focused. But just because this person is in you doesn't mean he or she is automatically going to come out. This person has to be released.

The apostle Paul gives us the secret in Romans 12:2. He said, "Be trans-formed by the renewing of your mind." In the original

> *Inside each of us is a blessed, prosperous, victorious person.*

language, the word *transformed* is *metamorphoo*. It's where we get our word *metamorphose*. We know how caterpillars metamorphose into butterflies. Paul is saying that if you'll get your thoughts going in the right direction and not dwell on negative, condemning, "not able to" thoughts, and program your mind with what God says about you, then a transformation will take place. When your thoughts are better, your life will be better.

Think about the caterpillar, the little wormlike larva that starts off as one of the most unattractive insects. It's very plain, nothing really special about it. But God predestined it to go through a transformation. At a certain point, it forms a cocoon, and metamorphosis starts to take place. It's a process. Little by little it changes. One day it begins to push out of the cocoon. A leg comes out, then a wing comes out. Soon, its head comes out. Before long, it's totally free from the cocoon. It has transformed from being one of the plainest insects into one of the most beautiful, colorful, and graceful—a butterfly. Instead of having to always crawl and squirm around on the ground, it can now fly to wherever it wants to go.

In a similar way, we all start off as worms, so to speak. Our thoughts, without being retrained, naturally gravitate toward the negative. We think, *I can't take that promotion. I'm not qualified.* Or, *I'll never rise much higher. I come from the wrong family.* Or, *I've made too many mistakes. God could never bless me.* You know what those are? Wormy thoughts. But just because we start out that way doesn't mean we're supposed to finish that way. God has predestined us to go through a transformation—from a wormlike larva that crawls and barely gets by to a beautiful butterfly that soars. Here's the key: It's not up to God; it's up to us. The only way to release your butterfly is to get your thinking in line with God's Word.

What will keep you in your cocoon? *I'll never lose this weight. My business isn't going to get off the ground. I'm not a good parent.* Those thoughts will keep the full you from coming out. You have to realize there is a great parent already in you just waiting to be released. If you're going to see your metamorphosis take place, you have to be convinced that "In me right now is a great father, a great mother. I'm going to renew my mind to get this person out." You may be struggling with an addiction, but in you right now is a person who is totally free. You may be down in your finances. Business is slow. But in you right now is a person who lends and does not borrow, who is the head and not the tail. If you will keep renewing your mind, agreeing with what God says about you, it's just a matter of time before that person comes out.

When thoughts tell you, *You're never going to change. It's never going to get any better*, just tell yourself, "I'm being transformed. My metamorphosis has already begun." That's how you release the full you. I know people who have incredible talent. They have so much to offer, but they've never gone through their transformation. They're allowing the same negative recording to play in their mind all day long. It's time to come out of your cocoon. God is ready to take you to a new level. He's ready to release a new wave of His favor. Now you have to rise up and say, "That's it. I'm done thinking wormy thoughts. It's my time to be transformed. I know I am forgiven. I am redeemed, talented, creative, and disciplined. I am well able."

That's not just being positive; that's renewing your mind. When you do that, I can see part of your wing coming out. I can see your leg breaking through the cocoon. You keep that

It's time to come out of your cocoon.

up and before long you'll release the full you. You'll be transformed into a beautiful butterfly soaring to places you never dreamed possible.

Transformation Takes Place as You Renew Your Mind

Robert grew up with a stepfather who always put him down. He was told again and again that he was slow and couldn't do anything right. "Why can't you be more like your brother?" Robert let those negative thoughts program his thinking and impact his living. He grew up very insecure, intimidated, with no dream for his life. When he graduated from high school, he got a job as a janitor at a small office complex. One day his mother remarried. This new stepfather was just the opposite. He constantly told Robert what he could become, how talented he was, and how there was a bright future in front of him. This stepfather spoke faith into him, helping to reprogram his thinking. He asked Robert what he wanted to do with his life, what his dream was.

Robert said, "I just want to work as a janitor at this office I'm at." He'd had years of wormy thoughts put into him. They don't go away overnight.

The stepfather said, "Robert, you have so much more in you. I'll make a deal with you. If you'll go to college, I'll pay for every book, every course, every meal, and every degree."

When Robert heard that, something came alive on the inside. Nobody had ever invested in him. Nobody had ever called out his seeds of greatness. He went to college, and in four years he got his bachelor's degree with honors. He decided to go on and get his master's, then his doctorate. But he wasn't finished. He went to seminary and received another degree. After four degrees, his stepfather said, "I'm done, Robert. You're on your own!" Today Robert is doing great things, living a life of victory, and helping others. But it would have never happened if he had not renewed his mind. He had to get rid of the wrong programming that had been put into him. When he started dwelling on the right thoughts—better thoughts of faith, victory, favor, and "can do"—that's when the transformation took place. He released his butterfly.

Maybe you've had negative things spoken over you just as Robert had. People told you what you can't do, what you're not going to become. Allow me to tell you who you really are. God says you are blessed. You are talented. You are valuable. You are confident. You have been handpicked by the Creator of the universe. Quit dwelling on what people say you are and program your mind with who God says you are.

On the inside of you right now is a victorious, successful world changer just waiting to break out. Your butterfly is waiting to soar! I'm asking you to release the full you. You are destined to leave your mark on your generation. There is no limit to what God can do in you and through you when you reprogram your thinking and start believing that you're blessed, valuable, one of a kind, and more than a conqueror. When you renew your mind, transformation takes place.

Your butterfly is waiting to soar!

Break Out of Your Cocoon

When I first started ministering back in 1999, I was so nervous. I didn't think I could do this. Every voice told me, "Joel, you better not get up there in front of people. You're going to make a fool of yourself. You're not going to know what to say. Nobody is going to listen to you." The enemy would have loved to keep me in my cocoon, thinking these wormy thoughts. He doesn't want you or me to break out and soar and live an overcoming life. He wants us to struggle, to be insecure, to be burdened by addictions and bad habits. It all starts in our mind. If he can control our thoughts, he can control our whole life.

I had to do what I'm asking you to do. All through the day I had to say, "I can do all things through Christ. I am strong in the Lord. If God be for me, who dare be against me?" I spoke those words month after month. Little by little, I started breaking out of my cocoon. A wing started to come out. The first couple of years I was so insecure that if I heard one negative comment, I would get discouraged. I would try to change and make sure everybody liked me. But as I continued to renew my mind and improve my thinking,

I realized I didn't need people's approval. I have Almighty God's approval.

What was happening? More of my wing was coming out. A little bit of my leg pushed through that cocoon. The truth is, I'm not totally transformed yet, but at least I'm not still in that cocoon. At least I'm not still crawling around thinking those wormy thoughts. When I compare myself now to where I started back then, in one sense I'm not the same person. I'm not nervous. I'm not insecure. I'm confident in who God made me to be. If somebody doesn't like me, it doesn't bother me the least bit. I'm happy. I'm blessed. My life is so much better. That's what it means to be transformed by the renewing of your mind.

Maybe you're not totally out of your cocoon yet either, but don't be discouraged. God is still working on you. Every day that you think the right thoughts, you are breaking out of that cocoon a little bit more. At the right time you're going to emerge completely and take off flying, and God is going to take you places you could never go on your own.

There was a man in the Scripture named Gideon. God wanted him to lead the people of Israel against an opposing army. But Gideon had all these wormy thoughts. He was stuck in his cocoon.

Every day that you think the right thoughts, you are breaking out of that cocoon a little bit more.

One day the Angel of the Lord appeared to him and said, "Hello, Gideon, you mighty man of fearless courage." I can imagine Gideon looking around thinking, *Who is He talking to? I am not a mighty man of fearless courage.* Gideon was just the opposite—he was afraid, intimidated, and insecure. But notice that God didn't call him what he was. God called him what he could become. God sees your potential. God knows what you're capable of. You may feel weak, but God calls you strong. You may be intimidated today, but God calls you confident. You may feel "less than," but God calls

you well able. If the Angel of the Lord were
to appear to you today, He would say the
same thing he said to Gideon. "Hello, you
mighty man, you mighty woman of fearless
courage."

Why don't you get in agreement with God
and start believing what He says about you?
Gideon answered the Angel, "How am I supposed to save Israel? I come from the poor-
est family in all of Manasseh, and I am the
least one in my father's house." Notice his
wormy thoughts. A lot of times, like Gideon,
we do the same thing. "I can't do anything
great. I'm not that talented. If only I was a
different nationality...If only I had a better personality...If only I hadn't made so
many mistakes..." Get rid of the excuses.
You are equipped. You are empowered. You
already have everything you need to fulfill
your destiny. It's in you right now, but you
have to do your part to bring it out.

See What You Can Become

I read about an older gentleman who was a well-known sculptor. He lived in a small hut on an island in the South Pacific. He was very talented and spent his whole life working with wood and carving different items. One day as he was walking by this beautiful plantation where the wealthiest man on the island lived, he saw several big tree trunks that had been cut down and piled in a big stack. He asked the owner what he was going to do with them. The owner said, "They're trash. They're useless. We're just going to haul them away."

"Do you mind if I take one of them?" the sculptor asked.

The owner looked at him kind of strange and said, "You want an old, dead piece of useless wood? Go ahead and take it."

The sculptor hauled the large section of tree trunk away in his wagon, got it to his hut, and stood it up inside the hut. He began to walk around it very slowly, carefully analyzing it, thinking about it, as if trying to release something that was trapped on the inside. A couple of hours later, he started carving away, whittling with precision, day after day. Two weeks went by, and he had carved the most beautiful eagle you could ever imagine. It was majestic looking, with its wings out, head back, soaring through the air. He put it on the front porch of his little hut.

One day the plantation owner walked by, saw the eagle, and was so impressed. He went up to it and marveled at the detail and how magnificent it was. He said to the man, "Where in the world did you get this? I'd like to buy it from you."

The sculptor chuckled and said, "No, sir. It's not for sale."

But the plantation owner was insistent. He said, "Name your price. I'll pay you whatever you want."

The sculptor finally said, "All right. How about five hundred dollars?"

The man paid him. Then, as the owner was walking away, the sculptor said, "Sir, I don't know if you realize it, but you just bought back the piece of useless wood you gave me several weeks ago."

The next day, the sculptor walked by the plantation. There was a sign out front that said, "Tree Trunks for Sale. $500 Each." The owner had learned his lesson.

Here's my point: The sculptor saw something in that discarded tree trunk that other people could not see. The plantation owner saw it as trash, useless, and of no value, but the sculptor was able to look beyond the rough exterior, beyond the flaws, and saw its potential. He knew what it could become.

It's the same way with our God. Your Creator can see things in you that other people cannot see. Sometimes people will try to push you down and make you feel insignificant. Sometimes our own thoughts will try to convince us we don't measure up. But God looks beyond the surface,

> *Look beyond your rough exterior, beyond your flaws, and see your potential.*

beyond the mistakes you've made, beyond what somebody said about you, and God sees your incredible value. You may think, *I've messed up. I've blown it. I've failed. I'm all washed up.* The good news is that God still sees the eagle in you. God doesn't just see what you are. He sees what you can become. People may have tried to push you down, but God sees you lifting up off the ground. He sees you soaring.

Now you have to do your part and get rid of those condemning thoughts. Get rid of what somebody has spoken over you and start renewing your mind. Down deep, start believing that you are redeemed, restored, talented, and valuable. God can still get you to where He wants you to be. Believe that you can still release the full you.

Royalty Is in You

In the Scripture, a man named Jacob had a lot of flaws. He was dishonest. He cheated people. He even tricked his own brother out of his birthright. He would be somebody we would compare to that discarded chunk of wood. Jacob didn't look as though he had much of a future, but God doesn't judge the way we judge. God doesn't look on the outside; He looks at the heart. Even when we make mistakes, God doesn't write us off. He always gives us another chance. Why? Because God can see the eagle in the tree trunk. He can see the butterfly in the worm. He can see a champion in a failure. But it's up to us. The only way the transformation will begin is for you to believe that you are forgiven, believe that there is mercy for every mistake, and believe that you are who God says you are.

One time in the Old Testament, an army invaded Jerusalem, kidnapped some of the people, and killed their king. For the first time, the people of Israel were without a leader. They were discouraged and didn't know what to do. As they sat there thinking that it was over, the prophet Micah rose up and said, "Why are you crying? Why are you discouraged? Is there not a king in you?"

I believe God is saying the same thing to each of us: "There's a king in you." You may have made mistakes, but the king is still in you. You may have gone through disappointments. People may have treated you unfairly. You missed good opportunities. But let these words sink deep down into your spirit. "The king is still in you." "The queen is still in you." You need to put your shoulders back, hold your head high, and carry yourself with confidence. You have royal blood flowing through your veins. You are wearing a crown of favor. I'm not talking to ordinary people. I'm talking to royalty. By faith, I can see kings. I can see queens. I can see your crown of favor. I can see your robe of honor. I'm talking to children of the Most High God. Now you have to start calling out that king, calling out that queen. You have to release what God put on the inside.

"Well, Joel, this is not for me. I've made lots of mistakes. I've lived a rough life." That didn't change what God put in you. You couldn't be any worse than Jacob. He failed again and again, but God's mercy is from everlasting to everlasting. It never runs out. God will never give up on you.

God kept working on Jacob, making him and molding him. One day God said, "Jacob, I'm going to change your name." His name literally meant "deceiver." God said, "I don't want you to be called that anymore. You've gone from a worm to a butterfly, from a discarded chunk of wood to a beautiful eagle. Your new name is going to be Israel." Israel means "prince with God." He went from being called a cheater to being called a king. After that, whenever somebody said, "Hello, Israel," they were saying, "Hello, King." They were calling out his seeds of greatness. They were prophesying, reminding him of who he really was. No doubt he started thinking better: *I'm not a cheater. I'm not a deceiver. I'm not a trickster. I'm a prince. I'm a king. I've been chosen by God. I have a destiny to fulfill. I have an assignment to accomplish.* He renewed his mind. That's when the transformation took place, and life suddenly improved greatly for Jacob.

Created to Soar

Could it be that the only things holding you back from a better life are your thoughts toward yourself? You're focused on your mistakes, how you blew it, how you didn't measure up. You have to reprogram your thinking. Get rid of the wormy thoughts. All through the day you should say, "I'm redeemed and restored. I am royalty. I am more than a conqueror."

I believe today is going to be the start of a transformation in your life. Some metamorphosis is about to take place. You need to get ready. Talent is going to come out of you that you didn't know you had. Strongholds of inferiority are being broken.

> *Get rid of the wormy thoughts.*

You're going to feel a new boldness, a new confidence to step into the fullness of your destiny. You may have one wing out, and that's good. But God doesn't want you to stay in your cocoon. He didn't create you to crawl and squirm. He created you to soar. It's time to get the other wing out. Keep thinking better thoughts. If you will start the renewing of your mind, programming it with what God says about you, you're going to release the full you.

I'm calling out the confident you. I'm calling out the successful you, the blessed you, the talented you, the disciplined you, the excellent you. I believe and declare the king in you is coming out. The eagle in you is coming out. The butterfly in you is coming out. You're not going to stay where you are. You're being transformed. You're going to soar to places that you could never have gone on your own. Receive it by faith!

CHAPTER FOUR

Think Yourself to Victory

Studies show that we talk to ourselves up to thirty thousand times a day. There is always something playing in our minds. The Scripture tells us to meditate on God's promises. The word *meditate* means "to think about over and over." We need to pay attention to what we're meditating on.

Meditating is the same principle as worrying. When you worry, you're just meditating on the wrong thing. You're using your faith in reverse. If you go through the day worried about your finances, worried about your family, and worried about your future, because you're allowing the wrong thoughts to play, it's going to cause you to be anxious, fearful, negative, and discouraged. The whole problem is what you're choosing to meditate on. You control the doorway to your mind. When those negative thoughts come knocking, you don't have to answer the door. You can say, "No, thanks. I'm going to choose to meditate on what God says about me."

Today, there is a lot of doom and gloom. If you watch the news for very long, you can get depressed—the stock market, the economy, the debt crisis. One phrase I observed in several newspapers was "total fear in the marketplace."

> *When you worry, you're just meditating on the wrong thing. You're using your faith in reverse.*

People are panicked. Some people go through their entire day thinking about how bad it is, asking themselves, "I wonder if I'm going to make it?" "What if I lose my job?" "What if my retirement funds go down?" If you dwell on these fearful thoughts, you're going to be stressed out. I like to watch the news, but I've learned not to meditate on the negative reports.

Philippians 4:8 says, "Think on things that are wholesome, things that are pure, things that are of good report." If it's not a good report, don't dwell on it, because it's going to poison your spirit. Instead of replaying the doom and gloom over and over, replay what God says. Yes, the financial situation may be a little shaky, but God says He will supply all your needs. He said He will prosper you even in a time of famine. He said He will open the windows of Heaven and pour out blessings that you cannot contain. Go through the day meditating on that. Get your mind going in the right direction. After all, the economy is not our source. God is our source. Our trust is not in the stock market or in the economy. I say it respectfully, but our trust is not even in the government. Our trust is in the Lord.

David said in one of his psalms, "Some trust in chariots. Some trust in horses. But our trust is in the name of the Lord our

God." In modern times, it would say, "Some trust in their money. Some trust in their job. Some trust in what the economists say. But our trust is in the God who created it all. He's called Jehovah Jireh, the Lord our Provider." When you meditate on that, you won't have total fear. You'll have total peace. You'll be at total rest. You know God is in control, and He can give you total victory. But it all depends on what's going on in your thought life. You can meditate on the problem or you can meditate on the promises. You can meditate on the news report or you can meditate on God's report. What you allow to play in your mind will determine what kind of life you live. When you think better, you will live better.

Perfect Peace

God said in Isaiah 26:3, "If you will keep your mind fixed on Me, I will keep you in perfect peace." Notice there is a way not only to have peace but to have perfect peace. How? Keep your thoughts fixed on Him. Pay attention to what is playing in your mind. You can't go through the day thinking, *I hope my child straightens up.* Or, *What's going to happen if I get laid off?* Or, *I might not overcome this illness.* When you dwell on thoughts such as these, you're not going to have peace. Meditating on the problem doesn't make it better; it makes it worse. You have to change what you're dwelling on. All through the day, go around thinking, *God has me in the palm of His hand. All things work together for my good. This problem didn't come to stay, it came to pass. Many are the afflictions of the righteous, but the Lord delivers me out of them all.* That's thinking better. When you meditate on that, you'll have greater peace, greater joy, and greater strength.

The apostle Paul understood this principle. He said, "I think myself happy." Happiness starts in our thinking. Paul had been through a lot of disappointments and hardships. He had been shipwrecked, put in jail, and mistreated, yet he wasn't focused on his problems. He wasn't meditating on how bad it was, replaying all his disappointments. He's the one who said, "Thanks be to God who always causes me to triumph. I am more than a conqueror." His mind was filled with thoughts of hope, thoughts of faith, thoughts of victory. He was saying, "It may look bad, but I've learned the secret of how to think myself happy."

Some people have thought themselves depressed. They have focused on their problems for so long they've thought themselves discouraged. They watched so many news reports they've thought themselves afraid. The good news is that just as you can think yourself depressed and fearful and negative, you can think yourself happy. You can think yourself peaceful. You can even think yourself into a better mood.

You can think yourself happy. You can think yourself peaceful..

The Scripture tells us, "Arise from the depression that has kept you down. Rise to a new life."

The first place in which we have to arise is our thinking. You have to put on a new attitude with better thoughts. Don't go through the day thinking about your problems, dwelling on who hurt you. That's going to keep you discouraged. You need to start thinking yourself happy. All through the day we should go around thinking, *My best days are in front of me. Something big is coming my way. What's meant for my harm, God is going to use to my advantage. My greatest victories are still in my future.* Purposefully think power thoughts: *I'm strong. I'm healthy. I'm blessed.* When you wake up in the morning and those thoughts come to you saying, *You don't want to go to work today. You have so many problems. You have so much coming against you,* more than ever, you need to kick it into gear. Counter those thoughts by declaring, "This is going to be a great day. This is the day the Lord has made. I'm excited about my future. Something good is going to happen to me today."

Here's the key: Don't ever start the day in neutral. You cannot wait to see what kind of day it's going to be. You have to *decide* what kind of day it's going to be. When you first get out of bed in the morning, before you check the news, before you check the weather, before you check to see how you feel, you need to set your mind in the right direction. "This is going to be a great day." If you don't set your mind, the enemy will set it for you. He will remind you of how bad you have it, how many mistakes you've made, and all the people who have come against you, on and on. Very often, the way we start the day will determine what kind of day we're going to have. If you start it nega-tive, discouraged, and complaining, you are setting the tone for a lousy day. You have to get your mind going in the right direction. Your life is going to follow your thoughts. If you get up thinking, *Nothing good ever hap-pens to me. I never get any breaks. I'll never get out of debt. I don't think I'll ever meet the right person and get married*, that's the direction in which you're releasing your faith.

You Become What You Believe

Jesus said, "Become what you believe." If you believe you'll never meet the right person and get married, unfortunately, you probably won't. Your faith is working. If you believe you'll never get out of debt, you won't. If you believe you're going to get laid off, don't be surprised if you do. You're going to become what you believe. I'm asking you to believe what God says about you. Believe that you are blessed. Believe that your best days are in front of you. Believe that you're strong, healthy, talented, creative, and well able. Get rid of those wrong thoughts that are contaminating your thinking, and start meditating on what God says about you.

The writer of Psalm 1 said, "If you will meditate on God's Word day and night, you will be like a tree planted by the water. Your leaf will not wither, but you will bear fruit in every season without fail." Notice that it is not in *some* seasons but in *every* season of your life. That means even if the economy goes down, you'll still be bearing fruit. It means that when others are going under, you'll be going over. When others have total fear, you'll have total peace. When others are complaining, you'll have a song of praise. When others are surviving, you'll be thriving.

The Message Bible translation says that when you meditate on God's Word, you will always be in blossom. That's God's dream for your life—that you always have a smile,

> *When others have total fear, you can have total peace.*

that you're always in peace, that you're always excited about your future. And no, it doesn't mean that we'll never have adversities. But in those difficult times, because you have your thoughts fixed on Him, deep down there will be a confidence, a knowing that everything is going to be all right. You will know that God is still on the throne. He is fighting your battles, and you're not only going to come out, you're going to come out better off than you were before.

I have friends who live in another state. The man works in sales for a large corporation. Recently he got the huge promotion that he had been hoping to receive for a long time. My friends were so excited, but it meant they had to move to a different city. The problem was that the housing market in their area was very down. Hardly anything was selling. They couldn't afford two house payments, so they had to sell their house before he could take the promotion. But instead of getting discouraged and thinking, *Just our luck, got the promotion at the wrong time. Our house is never going to sell*, they kept their minds filled with faith. All through the day they went around saying, "Father, You said Your favor surrounds us like a shield. You said we would always be in blossom. You said You would prosper us even in a famine." That's better thinking.

There were over sixty homes for sale in their neighborhood. In the previous seven months, only three houses had sold. It didn't look good, but they put their house on the market anyway; and two weeks later they had a contract to purchase their home. They talked to the new owners and out of curiosity asked them, "Why did you choose our house?"

The new buyers said, "We looked at over thirty houses in the neighborhood, but when we drove by your house, it just seemed to jump out at us. And when we went inside, we felt such a peace that we knew this was supposed to be our home."

That's what happens when you meditate on God's promises. You will always be in blossom. In other words, your property will sell when others are not selling. You'll get well when the medical report says you won't. You'll be promoted even though you're not the most qualified. Why is that? You have your mind filled with God's Word and know His thoughts toward you. When you're in agreement with God, the Creator of the universe goes to work. God will cause His favor to shine down on you. He will cause your house to stand out in the neighborhood. He will cause you to be at the right place at the right time, making sure that you succeed.

The bottom line is that you're going to become what you believe. Take inventory of what's playing in your mind. Don't go around thinking, *My house is never going to sell. You should see my neighborhood.* Or, *I'm afraid I'm never going to get well.* Or, *I'm afraid my child is going to go off on the wrong path.* Your faith is going to draw in the negative. Job said, "The thing I feared came upon me." Just as our faith can work in the right direction, it can work in the wrong direction.

Pay Attention to What Is Playing in Your Mind

I heard about this lady who bought a six-foot ficus tree for her bedroom. She loved plants, had them all over her house, and was very experienced at taking care of them. But the next morning, she woke up and thought to herself, *This plant is not going to make it. It's not going to live.* That negative thought came out of the blue, and she made the mistake of dwelling on it, thinking about it over and over. She even told her husband, "I think I've wasted my money on this plant. I'm just afraid it's not going to live."

"What are you talking about?" he asked. "All your plants have lived. Why would you say that?"

"Oh," she said, "something just tells me it's not going to make it."

Three weeks later, for no apparent reason, the leaves on the plant started to turn yellow. A few days later, the leaves had all fallen off. A few weeks later, the plant had totally withered up, completely dead.

One day she was thinking about that dead tree. She sensed God spoke something to her, not out loud but an impression on the inside. He said, "I want you to know you killed that plant with your thoughts."

When she heard that, chills went up and

down her spine. When we dwell on the negative, we're releasing our faith in the wrong direction. She told her husband, "I know you're going to think I'm crazy, but I think I killed this plant with my thoughts."

He looked at her very strangely and replied, "All I can say is that I hope you're thinking good thoughts about me."

Pay attention to what's playing in your mind. I'm not saying that every negative thought is going to come to pass; my point is that we can open the door to difficulties by dwelling on the wrong things.

Fill Your Mind with the Right Thoughts

I've learned that if you fill your mind with the right thoughts, there won't be any room for the wrong thoughts. When you go around constantly thinking, *I'm strong. I'm healthy. I'm blessed. I have the favor of God*, then when the negative thoughts come knocking, there will be a "No Vacancy" sign. "Sorry, no room for you." They won't be able to get in.

Once when I was traveling with my father to India, our plane was delayed because of bad weather. We missed our connecting flight in Europe, and since it was late at night, we went to a hotel at the airport. We walked straight to the front desk, and my father asked the young hotel clerk for a room.

The young man checked the computer and said, "Sorry, sir. We're totally full tonight."

My dad wasn't about to take no for an answer. He said politely, "Can you please look again? We're really tired."

The young man checked and checked. Again he said, "I'm sorry, but we have no vacancy. We're totally full."

My father asked to speak to the manager, who came out and went through the same procedure; he even went to his office to do an additional check but finally came back and said, "Sir, I'm so sorry. We don't have any rooms."

Dad said, "We're just going to be here a few hours. Can't we have some place to stay?"

The manager looked at my father and said, "Sir, I can't make anyone leave the hotel. We are totally full."

That's how it is when you keep your mind filled with God's Word. A thought of fear comes knocking: *You're not going to make it. The problem is too big. Let me in. Give me a room to stay.* But just like that hotel manager, you declare, "Sorry, fear, there's no vacancy. No room. You're going to have to go somewhere else to stay."

That thought that sows doubt, *You'll never sell your house. Have you seen the market?* "No vacancy. God's favor surrounds me like a shield."

You'll never get well. Have you seen the medical report? "No vacancy. God is restoring health to me."

You've seen your best days. "No vacancy. This mind is filled with better thoughts of faith, hope, victory, increase, abundance, and restoration. There's no room for doubt, unbelief, anxiety, fear, or depression."

You need to take inventory of who is staying in your house. Who is occupying your rooms? If you give fear a room, faith gets left outside. There's not room for both. If you give "I can't" a room, "I can" is left outside. If you give lack, barely get by, "I'll never make it" a room, then increase, promotion, and abundance are left outside. Get rid of the wrong thoughts and let what God says about you have a permanent home.

Think of it like this. Before you go to bed at night, you lock the doors to your house. You don't want any strangers coming in. That's where you live. That's your home. You need to have that same thinking when it comes to your mind. "This is where I live. This is who I am. This is my future. I'm not going to let just any thought come in and have a permanent home. I'm going to guard the

You need to take inventory of who is staying in your house.

doorway to my mind and only give a room to thoughts of hope, thoughts of faith, and thoughts of victory."

I've heard it stated like this: If you owned an apartment complex and you rented 80 percent of the apartments to drug dealers, thieves, and cheaters, and you rented the other 20 percent to good, law-abiding citizens, after a few months the drug dealers and cheaters would run off all the good people. It's the same way with our thoughts. If you go around thinking about how bad things are, dwelling on your problems, all that you don't have, and how tough your future is going to be, all those negative thoughts are going to run off any positive thoughts and limit how you live. You have to quit renting out space in your mind to your problems. Quit renting out valuable space to self-pity. Don't rent it out to can't-do-it, not-going-to-happen thoughts. You only have so much space in your mind. Maybe you need to serve an eviction notice. Tell those negative thoughts, "You've occupied my rooms long enough. I've got a new renter coming in. My new renter is faith, joy, peace, and healing. My new tenant is victory."

People Do Not Have the Final Say

I'm not saying to deny the negative reports that are true and to act as though they don't exist. I'm simply saying: Don't dwell on them. Don't let them consume you to where that's all you think and talk about. Learn to put things in perspective.

One time in the Scripture, Jesus was on His way to pray for a person who was very sick, but He kept getting delayed. Finally, people from the sick person's house came and said, "Tell Jesus He doesn't need to come any longer. It's too late. The person has already died." Jesus was standing very close by. The Scripture says Jesus, "overhearing, but ignoring," heard the negative report, but He didn't let it take root. He didn't meditate on it. He didn't get discouraged. He didn't turn around and go back home. He didn't deny that the report was true or pretend the person had not died.

Jesus knew people don't have the final say. God has the final say. Sometimes in order to stay in faith you have to ignore a negative report. You have to ignore what somebody said about you. You have to ignore what your own thoughts are telling you. You may hear it, but you can do like Jesus and choose not to dwell on it.

When our children were younger, occasionally one of their friends would be talking too much, and if they didn't want to hear any more, they would put out an arm and say, "Talk

Sometimes in order to stay in faith you have to ignore a negative report.

to the hand." That meant, "You're talking, but I'm not listening." That's what we need to do when negative thoughts come. In your imagination, just extend your arm and say, "Talk to the hand. You're talking, but I'm not listening to you. You're trying to rent a room, but I'm telling you, 'No vacancy here.'"

I was watching a football game several years ago. It was a very important playoff game. There were only a few seconds left on the clock. The visiting team was down by two points, and they were setting up to attempt a field goal to win the game. The kicker was on the field, lining up, getting ready for the biggest kick of his life. The opposing fans were hollering at him so loud, screaming, jeering, trying to distract him. Just as he was about to kick, the other team called a timeout to give the fans more time to try and intimidate him. On the stadium's big screen, they started playing video clips of all the times this kicker had missed in the past. Going back many years, they replayed all his failures, and every time he missed, the whole crowd went crazy. With eighty thousand people screaming against him, he stepped up and kicked the ball right through the uprights and won the game.

Afterward a reporter asked him how he could handle the pressure with so many thousands of people screaming against him. He said, "I didn't hear anybody screaming. I just kept telling myself, 'You can do this. You have what it takes.'"

The reporter said, "Well, what about on the big screen when they were replaying all your failures?"

"I saw that," he answered with a smile, "but I didn't pay any attention. I just ignored it."

In life there will be times when it feels as though every voice is telling you, "You can't do it. It's not going to work out. You'll never overcome this problem." It may be the voices of the people around you, the critics, the naysayers. Or it may just be voices in your mind, thoughts trying to discourage you. Don't be surprised if the enemy even starts replaying your failures, replaying the times when you've missed it, replaying all your disappointments. You have to do what this young kicker did. Choose to ignore it, and choose to believe a better report. If you will get in agreement with God and not let those distractions pull you off course, God will get you to where He wants you to be.

Victory Starts in Your Thinking

Friend, the first place we lose the victory is in our own thinking. You may feel as though eighty thousand voices are screaming against you right now, saying, "It's never going to work out. This problem is too big. You might as well just settle where you are."

Put your hand out. Tell those negative thoughts, "Talk to the hand." If they want to rent a room, show them the "No Vacancy" sign. If you'll keep your thoughts fixed on what God says, you will overcome the obstacles and accomplish your dreams. That's what it says in Joshua 1:8: "If you will meditate on God's Word day and night, you will prosper and have good success."

The whole key is what's going on in your thought life. What are you meditating on?

Make a decision that you're going to keep your thoughts fixed on what God says. Purposefully think power thoughts: *I'm strong. I'm talented. I'm creative. I have the favor of God.* Remember, you're going to become what you believe.

When you get up every morning, set your mind in the right direction. Don't meditate on the problem. Meditate on the promises. Learn to think yourself happy. Think yourself peaceful.

The whole key is what's going on in your thought life.

Think yourself victorious. Victory starts in your thinking.

CHAPTER FIVE

Pregnant with Possibility

When a woman is pregnant, for the first few months she typically doesn't look any different. She's the same size, wears the same clothes, and has the same amount of energy. From the outside, there's no sign that she's going to have a baby. If you just looked at it in the natural, you could think, *She's not pregnant. There's nothing different about her.* But what you can't see is that on the inside a seed has taken root. Conception has occurred. A few months into the pregnancy, she'll start showing, gaining more weight. Weeks later, she'll feel something kicking on the inside. Suddenly a kick here, a kick there. She's still never seen the baby in person. She's never held that baby, but she's not worried, because she knows the baby is on the way. Nine months after she conceives, she'll give birth to that little child.

In a similar way, you may not realize it, but you are pregnant. God has placed all kinds of potential in you. There are gifts, talents, and ideas. He's put dreams, businesses, books, songs, healing, and freedom inside you. You are pregnant with possibilities, pregnant with increase, pregnant with healing. Just because you don't see anything happening doesn't mean it's not going to come to pass. The seed God put in you has already taken root. Conception has occurred.

As was true for this woman, you may not see any sign of the pregnancy at the begin-ning, but don't worry. Your time is coming. You are pregnant with your miracle, pregnant with abun-dance. Maybe you're

> *Just because you don't see anything happening doesn't mean it's not going to come to pass.*

pregnant with a new business. Instead of being discouraged and thinking, *It's never going to happen. It's been so long. I've been through too much,* your attitude should be, *I can feel something kicking on the inside. I know something good is growing. I'm going to give birth to what God put in me.*

Maybe you've struggled with an addiction for a long time. Instead of believing the lie that says you can never break free, say, "No, I'm pregnant with freedom. I'm pregnant with wholeness. You may not see any changes in me, but I can feel something kicking. I can feel something stirring down in my spirit." When you live with this kind of expectancy, you're going to give birth to what God put in you.

Something Is Kicking on the Inside

Psalm 7 says, "The ungodly are pregnant with trouble." The good news is: That's not you. You are the righteous. You're not pregnant with trouble, with bad breaks, sickness, lack, or depression. You are pregnant with favor, pregnant with talent, pregnant with victory. All through the day, keep saying, "Lord, I thank You that I'm pregnant with Your promises, that I will give birth to everything You've put in me." You may not see any changes. It may not look in the natural as though it's ever going to work out, but deep down in your spirit, you choose to believe that conception has occurred. You are pregnant with that new house you've been dreaming about. In God's perfect timing, when everything is ready, you're going to give birth.

Your family may be struggling with dysfunction in your home. Don't live worried. You are pregnant with restoration, pregnant with the breakthrough. Maybe business is slow and you lost your main client. You could easily be discouraged, but you can feel something kicking on the inside, something saying, "You are the head and not the tail. Whatever you touch will prosper and succeed." Perhaps your dream looks impossible.

It's been a long time, you gave it your best effort, and it didn't work out; but deep down you can't help it—something keeps kicking, telling you that it's still on the way. What God started, He will finish.

I talked to a gentleman recently who was diagnosed with cancer. The doctors told him it was a very invasive type that would spread quickly to other areas. After the scheduled surgery, he was going to have to take one year of chemotherapy. The prognosis didn't look good, but he didn't get depressed. He didn't go around saying, "Why me, God?" He understood the principle that he was pregnant with healing. The doctors performed the surgery. Afterward they came into his hospital room scratching their heads. They had been certain it was a very dangerous invasive type of cancer, but when they retested it, it wasn't what they had thought. They were able to remove all the cancer, he didn't need any more treatment, and today he's totally cancer-free.

You may be struggling with an illness,

fighting a battle in your health. Instead of accepting the illness, thinking that's the way it's always going to be, keep reminding yourself that you are pregnant. You've already conceived. The healing is already in you. It's just a matter of time before you give birth. Nothing can snatch you out of God's hands. Don't go around negative and complaining. Turn it around with better thoughts. "The medical report doesn't look good, but I can feel healing kicking on the inside of me. No weapon formed against me will prosper." Or, "It doesn't look as though I can ever get out of debt, but I can feel abundance kicking on the inside. I will lend and not borrow." Or, "All my circumstances say that I'll be barren my whole life, never meet the right person, never break the addiction, but deep down I can feel something stirring in my spirit."

Realize that you are pregnant with possibility. Quit telling yourself that you can never get ahead, that you don't have enough of this, enough of that. You are pregnant with success, pregnant with ideas, pregnant with your destiny. You're going to give birth to what God put in you. It's not too late. You haven't missed your chance.

> *You are pregnant with success, pregnant with ideas, pregnant with your destiny.*

Don't Go By What You See in Your Circumstances

In the Scripture, Sarah was over ninety years old when she gave birth to Isaac. This is way too old in the natural, but we serve a supernatural God. He can make a way where you don't see a way. Don't abort your baby. Don't talk yourself out of your dreams. Don't give up on what God promised you. You can still give birth. You can still meet the right person, still start your own business, still go to college, still break the addiction. That seed is alive in you.

Here's the key: You can't judge what's in you by what's around you. All of Sarah's circumstances said, "You'll be barren your whole life. You're too old. No woman your age has babies. It's impossible." If she had believed that lie, let that seed take root, the miracle birth would never have happened. You can draw in the negative with your doubt or you can draw in God's blessings with your faith. Don't let what you see around you cause you to give up on your dreams.

I was in a large city recently. Part of the city was very beautiful, but another part was very run-down. There were miles and miles of abandoned homes, and people living next door to boarded-up houses. When we drove through this neighborhood during the daytime, there were hundreds, if not thousands, of people outside—young and old, just hanging out, with no apparent purpose, no direction. For most of these people, that's all they've ever known. They were born into it. They grew up in the projects, living in the midst of drugs, dysfunction, and violence.

You may be in some kind of limited

environment today, with nothing inspiring around you. In the natural, there's no obvious way that you can get out, get an education, and become successful, but what's around you does not determine what God put in you. You have seeds of greatness. You are pregnant with success, pregnant with ability, pregnant with talent. God did not create anyone in whom He did not put something significant on the inside. Don't let what's on the outside—how you were raised, the lack, the dysfunction—convince you to abort your dream. When you get quiet, alone at night, when it's just you and God, if you listen carefully, you'll hear something whispering, "This is not your destiny. You were made for more." What is that? That's your baby kicking. It's because you're going to give birth. You're going to see supernatural

You were made for more.

opportunities, explosive blessings, and divine connections. God is going to help you go where you could not go on your own.

You Can Be the Barrier Breaker

This is what happened to my father. Statistics during the Great Depression said he would have to stay on the farm and pick cotton the rest of his life. Nobody in his family had done anything different. But statistics don't determine your destiny; God does. Don't become a victim of your environment. Where you are is not who you are.

Daddy told me, "Joel, when I was seventeen years old, I made the decision that my children would never be raised in the poverty and lack that I was raised in." What happened? He became pregnant. He could feel that baby kicking on the inside. But if someone were to have studied my father in that limited environment, they would've said, "John, there's nothing special about you. You're not going to do anything great." In other words, "You're not pregnant. There's no sign on the outside. You're not showing. You look just the same." But what they couldn't see was that conception had already occurred. My father looked the same on the outside, but on the inside a seed had taken root. He knew he was destined to leave his mark on his generation. He didn't let people talk him out of it. He didn't let his environment hold him back. He had better thoughts. He kept praying, believing, and taking steps of faith. He gave birth to everything God put in him.

As was true for my father, the odds may be stacked against you. The medical report doesn't look good or your environment is not healthy. Nobody's supporting you, and you don't have the connections or the resources to get yourself there. Don't talk yourself out of it. Keep reminding yourself that you are pregnant. The seed put in you by your Creator has already taken root. It doesn't have anything to do with what you have or don't have, what family you come from, or how talented you are. It is a destiny seed. When you give birth, you're going to go further than you ever imagined.

Sarah was eighty years old and had never

had a baby when God told Abraham he would have a son as an heir. Everywhere she looked it said that she would be barren her whole life. She couldn't find another eighty-year-old woman who had ever had a baby. If she could have found at least one, she could've said, "God, You did it for her. You can do it for me." But she couldn't find anyone.

You may look around and think, *I don't know anyone who's gotten out of my neighborhood and done something significant. I don't know anyone who's overcome the illness I'm dealing with. Nobody in my family has been able to break these addictions.* The good news is you can be the first. You can set the new standard. You can be the barrier breaker.

God said in effect to Sarah, "I will give you a son. You will be the mother of nations. Kings of people will come out of you." Here's an eighty-year-old woman who's barren. She's living in the desert, with no medical procedures and no infertility treatments available, yet God says, "You have kings in you. You have nations in you." He was saying, "Sarah, don't let the circumstances fool you. Don't let your environment talk you out of it. Don't let your own thoughts discourage you. You are pregnant with greatness." God is saying the same thing to you. "You have kings in you. You have greatness in you. You are pregnant with success. Pregnant with talent. Pregnant with your destiny."

Wake Up!

The prophet Joel said, "Wake up the mighty men, wake up the mighty women!" I'm here to wake up your dreams, wake up your talents, wake up your potential, wake up what God put in you. You may have let some circumstances convince you that it's never going to happen, but I believe you're going to start feeling some kicking on the inside. That baby, that dream, that promise is still alive in you. You better get ready. You're going to give birth to something that's going to take you further than you could ever imagine. It's going to thrust you to a new level of your destiny.

A lady told me how she had had a stroke. She'd been in a hospital for three weeks and finally was able to go back home, but she was very depressed. She didn't think she'd ever be able to walk again. She lost

> *You're going to give birth to something that's going to take you further than you could ever imagine.*

her passion, lost her drive. But the Scripture talks about fighting the good fight of faith. You can't be passive and just accept whatever comes along and think that's your lot in life. We all have bad breaks and disappointments. Those challenges are not there to defeat you; they're there to promote you. On the other side is a new level of God's goodness. But you have to do your part and get your fire back.

One Sunday this lady heard me on television talking about how God wants to restore what's been stolen, how He can give you beauty for ashes, how you can still live healthy and whole. Those are better thoughts. When she heard that, she said, something woke up in her spirit. Something came alive on the inside. What happened? That baby started kicking. She was already pregnant with healing. God already had the restoration there, but when her spirit came alive, when she started believing, that's when things began to change. Instead of going around thinking, *I'll never walk again. I'll never get well*, she started declaring, "I am healthy. I am strong. I am well able. I am restored." Against all the odds, she started walking again. She's getting stronger and healthier. It all started when something woke up in her spirit.

Maybe, like her, you've let something steal your passion. You don't think you will ever get well, ever meet the right person, ever accomplish a dream. Recognize that everything you need is already in you. If you'll stir your faith up as she did and get in agreement with God, you will give birth to your healing, birth to your dreams, birth to those promises. Genesis 3:15 says, "The seed of the woman will bruise the head of the serpent." You remember how the serpent deceived Eve in the Garden of Eden and brought about all kinds of trouble. God was saying in effect, "Eve, it's payback time. You're going to give birth to something that's going to defeat the thing that's tried to defeat you. Your seed will bruise his head."

Too often we're looking for something from the outside to help us overcome, but God has put it on the inside. Give birth to what God put in you, and stop relying on other people. If you'll give birth to that dream, that gift, that talent, as my father did, your gift will make room for you. Your gift will open some new doors. If you'll give birth to that idea, that book, or that potential, you can deliver yourself from lack and struggle. Jesus said, "Out of your belly will flow rivers of living water." Your deliverance is not going to come from other people. Your promotion, your healing, your breakthrough is going to come from within you. Out of your belly shall flow rivers.

Recognize the True Labor Pains

"Well, Joel, I believe I'm pregnant. I have big dreams, and I'm standing on God's promises, but everything is coming against me. It seems as though the more I pray, the worse it gets. I'm doing the right thing, but the wrong thing is happening." Here's the beauty: Pain is a sign that you're about to give birth. Trouble, difficulties, being uncomfortable—those are signs that you're getting closer.

When Victoria was pregnant with our two children, the first couple months were no big deal, everything was fine. But about seven or eight months in, her back began hurting, her feet started swelling, and she couldn't sleep well at night. The longer she was pregnant, the more uncomfortable

Pain is a sign that you're about to give birth.

she became. When she went into labor, I was in the delivery room right next to her bed, and she had her hand on my bicep. When she had a contraction, it would hurt so badly she would squeeze my arm as hard as she could. She would scream, then I would scream. The closer she got to the birth, the more painful it was. When everything comes against you—your child's acting up, trouble at work, setbacks in your finances—don't get discouraged. You're about to give birth. You're about to see a promise come to pass.

It is during the tough times that many people abort their dreams, thinking, *I knew it wouldn't work out. The bank turned me down. The medical report wasn't good. I didn't get the promotion.* Recognize that those are labor pains. You're getting closer. Stay in faith. Keep doing the right thing. The birth is on the way.

I heard a story about a young couple out hiking through the woods when they came upon a large patch of wild mushrooms. They decided to take some home and cook them.

They had friends over for dinner that night. One of the side dishes was the sautéed mushrooms. At one point the large family cat, which loved to eat, came into the room. The husband grabbed some mushrooms and fed them to the cat, which ate them as though they were dessert. About an hour later, he heard the cat making a strange sound. He ran into the other room to check on her; she was lying flat on her back, foaming at the mouth, in intense pain. He called the veterinarian, who asked, "What has the cat eaten recently?"

"Wild mushrooms," the man said, feeling a bit of panic, "but we've all eaten them, too."

"They may be poisonous," the vet stated. "You'd better go to the emergency room and get checked out immediately."

The man and all his guests rushed to the emergency room. A few hours later, when they arrived back at the house, the man went in to check on the cat, thinking that she would be knocked out. Instead, the cat was lying calmly on her side with the seven kittens she had just birthed.

Sometimes what we think is a setback is really just labor pains. That difficulty you're facing is not the end; it's a part of the birthing process. You're about to step into a new level of your destiny. Don't be discouraged by the disappointment, the closed door, or the bad break. That's a sign you're about to give birth to something greater.

> *Sometimes what we think is a setback is really just labor pains.*

Keep Believing, Keep Doing

I read about a gentleman who was having a tough time paying his bills. He'd had a rough childhood. At the age of two, his father went to the store to buy groceries and never returned home, leaving his mother to raise two small children on her own. In college, he met and fell in love with his wife, but he was so poor he had to borrow a suit and tie for his wedding. He and his wife had a newborn baby, and they were living in an old, run-down trailer. He drove a rusted-out car that was held together with wire and duct tape. In the summers, during the day he worked for a laundry company, making sixty dollars a week. At night, he worked as a janitor, cleaning offices. He had a dream to become a writer, but he couldn't afford a typewriter. He had to use his wife's portable typewriter from college and set it up in their small laundry room. When he wasn't working, he would spend hour after hour writing fiction stories. He sent manuscripts of his novels to different publishers and agents, but every one of them was rejected. He didn't even know if people were actually reading them. He began writing one final story, but he was so discouraged that he threw the manuscript in the trash. His wife came home and found it crumpled up in the garbage, took it out, and eventually they sent that story to a different publisher. This time the publisher responded and offered him a contract. That story went on to sell over five million books. In 1976, it was made into a movie and became one of the top-grossing films of the year. That young man was Stephen King, one of the most successful writers of our day.

Like him, some of you are pregnant with a book, pregnant with a movie, pregnant with a business, or maybe pregnant with a charity. You've had disappointments—you tried and it didn't work out—but you can still feel the kicking on the inside. You can't get away from it. Don't talk yourself out of it. It's all a part of the process. Keep trying, keep believing, keep doing everything you can, and at the right time you will give birth. The right people, the right opportunities, and the right breaks will show up. You can't make it happen on your own; it will be the hand of God. What He's put in you is going to be bigger than you could have imagined, better than anything you've ever dreamed, and more rewarding than you ever thought possible.

Get your hopes up. Every morning, remind yourself that you are pregnant—and not with rejection, failure, disappointments, and defeat. You are pregnant with victory, pregnant with success, pregnant with the favor of God. Sure, you may have had some bad breaks, but as with Sarah, you are not going to live your life barren, you're not going to die with that baby still in you. God has the final say, and He says a birth is coming; what He's promised is on the way. Keep honoring Him, keep being your best, and I believe and declare you will give birth to everything God put in you and become everything God created you to be.

CHAPTER SIX

The Promise Is in You

So often, we look at others and think, *Wow, they are so amazing, and I am so ordinary.* Or we'll say, "My cousin is so beautiful, but I'm so plain." We come home from the office and tell our spouse, "My coworker is so smart, and I'm so average." While it's true that they may be amazing in certain areas, you have to realize there's something amazing about you as well. You are talented, you are attractive, and you have been fearfully and wonderfully made. God doesn't want us to go around just celebrating others, cheering them on, although that's good. God wants you to be celebrated as well. You didn't get left out when God was handing out the gifts, the talents, or the looks. He put something in you that will cause you to shine. You can be a great businessperson, a great entrepreneur, a great teacher, a great mother. Don't get so focused on what somebody else has that you don't realize what you have.

During World War II, the famous actress Betty Grable was known for her beautiful legs. Her studio had them insured with Lloyd's of London for $1 million. That was unheard-of back then—a pair of legs worth a million dollars. Do you want to see another pair of million-dollar legs? Look down at your own. If somebody offered you a million dollars to buy your legs, you wouldn't take it.

You have to realize there's something amazing about you as well.

A few years ago, a man lost his arm in an accident. The court awarded him $11 million for that arm. Look at your arm. It's worth $11 million. In another city, a young lady injured her back while riding in a city bus and lost her ability to work. The city awarded her $20 million. Think about it. Just those three things and you're already worth $32 million. You're starting to feel better about yourself, aren't you? Sometimes we're always celebrating others, but God is saying that it's time to celebrate yourself. There's something special about you.

It's Time to Step Up

For many years, I cheered my father on. Daddy was my hero. When I was a little boy, we used to travel to different cities, and I'd see my father up on the platform, speaking to thousands of people. He was so warm and friendly. Everybody loved him. I was so proud that he was my father. In the back of my mind, I thought, *I could never do that. He's so gifted. He's so talented.* After I came back from college, I worked for seventeen years behind the scenes at the church with my parents, doing the television production.

Week after week, I'd watch my father on
the platform, ministering, making a difference, doing something great. I did my best
to make my father look good. I made sure
the camera angles were just right and the
lighting was just perfect. I would even go
over to his house on Saturday night and pick
out a suit and tie for him to wear the next
morning for television at the church services.

As my father got older, people would ask,
"Joel, what's going to happen when your dad
goes to be with the Lord? Who's going to
pastor the church?" My father had never des-
ignated or trained a successor. Over the years,
he tried many times to get me to minister,
but I didn't think that was in me. However, when he died in 1999, all of a sudden
I had a strong desire to step up and pastor the church. I'd never ministered or been
to seminary. Yet deep down, I heard a still
small voice saying, "Joel, you've spent your
whole life celebrating others. Now it's time
for you to be celebrated. It's time for you
to step up to a new level of your destiny." I

always knew that God would take care of the church after my dad was gone, but I never dreamed it would be through me. I thought the promise would happen some other way, but I discovered the promise was in me.

God is saying the same thing to you. You've celebrated others. Now it's time to celebrate yourself. It's time for you to think better thoughts about yourself. It's time for you to shine. There is a seed on the inside just waiting to flourish. You may not feel as though you can do it, but God would not have given you the opportunity unless He had

There is a seed on the inside just waiting to flourish.

already equipped and empowered you. You have everything you need.

The Promise Comes Through You

I heard about a minister who, before a morning service, handed a man a hundred-dollar bill and asked him to place it secretly in his wife's Bible and make sure she didn't see it. They were all friends, so the man went along with it.

During the sermon, the minister asked this man's wife to stand up. He said to her, "Do you trust me?"

She smiled and said, somewhat hesitantly, wondering what he was up to, "Yes...I do."

"Will you do what I ask?"

She continued her quizzical look and nodded, then said, "Yes, I will."

"Then open your Bible and give me a hundred-dollar bill."

"Oh, I'm so sorry," she offered with a shake of her head. "I don't have a hundred-dollar bill."

"Do you trust me?" the minister pressed a bit more.

"Yes, I do."

"Will you do what I ask?"

"Yes, I will."

"Then open your Bible and hand me a hundred-dollar bill."

Reluctantly, she opened her Bible, and much to her surprise, she saw the money. She shook her head again, laughing out loud, and asked, "How did it get there?"

The minister smiled and said, "I put it in there."

In the same way, God will never ask you for something without first putting it in you. When God gives you a dream, when you have a desire and you know you're supposed to take a step of faith, you may feel completely unqualified. You may tell yourself that you don't have the wisdom, the know-how, or the ability to take the step. But if you'll dare to take that step, just as I did, you'll discover things in you that you never knew you had. I never knew the gift to minister was in me. I never knew that I could get up in front of people and minister

How many gifts are in you right now just waiting to be released?

to them. I wonder how many gifts are in you right now just waiting to be released.

This is where Sarah, Abraham's wife, almost missed it. She thought the promise from God would come through somebody else. God told her that she was going to do something great. She was going to have a child at an old age and her husband would become the father of many nations. She said, "God, that's impossible. I'm eighty years old. That's never happened. I must not be hearing You right." Thinking it couldn't happen through her, Sarah took matters into her own hands. She had Abraham sleep with one of her maids, Hagar, and they had a son named Ishmael. Sarah looked and said, "There he is, the child of promise."

God replied, "No, Sarah, I didn't say the promise was in somebody else. I said the promise is in you. You spent your whole life celebrating others, but now it's time for you to be celebrated. You're going to give birth. You're going to have that baby. You're going to be a history maker." Those were the better thoughts she should have believed in the first place, which would have helped them avoid so many family problems with Ishmael. Sure enough, when Sarah was over ninety years old, just as God had said, she gave birth to that baby. The promise was fulfilled.

What God has placed in your heart is not going to come to pass through your neighbor, your cousin, your coworker, your friend, or your parents. God is saying, "I've anointed you. I've equipped you. I've breathed My life into you." Now quit looking for somebody else. Quit thinking that you don't have what it takes. You've been chosen by the Creator of the universe. You don't need anyone else to give birth to the promise that God put in your heart.

You Are the Right Person

Dr. Todd Price is a friend of mine. He grew up very poor in a small town. It didn't look as though he had much of a future. But from the time he was a little boy, he had a desire to help children in need. One day he saw a program on television describing how you could sponsor a needy child in a third-world country for fifteen dollars a month. He didn't have any money, but his heart was so moved that he started mowing lawns and doing yard work in the neighborhood to raise the money. When he was just twelve years old, he started sponsoring a little girl who lived halfway around the world. What caused him to do that? Why did he have that compassion? It was the promise God put in him. It was a seed of greatness just waiting to be developed.

Dr. Price wasn't raised in a religious home, but every night before he went to bed, he'd say, "God, please send some wealthy person to help these children in need." He was able to go to college, and during the summers, he took trips overseas with a group of doctors to treat needy children. When he looked in their eyes, he would pray even more earnestly, "God, please send some wealthy person to help these children." He was able to find a way to go to medical school, and he continued going overseas. Eventually, he became a doctor and started his own medical practice. One of his main suppliers heard that he helped needy children and asked if he could use free medical supplies, vaccinations, and antibiotics. Of course he could, and soon Dr. Price started taking a couple suitcases full of medicines on each trip. It grew to where he had to put the medical supplies in boxes and have them shipped. Eventually, it expanded so abundantly that he was shipping huge containers of medicines overseas. All the while, he kept praying, "God, please send some wealthy person to help these children in need."

In the last few years, Dr. Price's medical missions organization, International Medical Outreach, has treated over fifty million children in twenty-one countries. He has provided nearly a billion dollars' worth of medicines and supplies. He said, "About two years ago, when I was treating my twentieth million child, I finally realized that God had answered my prayers. But it wasn't like

I thought. I always prayed for God to send some wealthy person. Now I realize I am that wealthy person." He was saying, "The promise is in me."

You don't need anyone else to give birth to what God has placed in your heart. Maybe you're waiting for the *right* person. God is saying, "You are the right person. My anointing is on your life. My favor is on your life. You're equipped and empowered. You can do something great." Now, don't do as Sarah did and say, "Okay, God, let me go find somebody younger, somebody smarter, more educated, and more talented." You

> *Don't miss your destiny waiting for somebody else.*

have what it takes. Don't miss your destiny waiting for somebody else.

God Doesn't Change His Mind

When my father went to be with the Lord, in the back of my mind I thought that God would send us a senior pastor with a dynamic personality and a booming voice and several academic degrees behind his name. I was looking around, thinking, *Where is he?* The whole time, on the inside I could hear that still small voice saying, "Joel, this is your time. This is your moment. The promise is in you." I said, "God, I don't have the booming voice. I don't have the dynamic personality. I don't have the degrees." God said, "Joel, I formed you before the foundation of the world. I put in you everything that you need. I wouldn't ask you to do it if you didn't already have what it takes." I stepped up, and as Dr. Price did, I discovered *I* was the answer to my prayer. Maybe you're praying for another person to come along and bring your dreams to pass. God is saying, "You're the answer to your prayer. You're equipped and anointed; you can do something great."

As with Sarah, just because we don't believe it's going to happen, God doesn't change His mind. Sarah waited a dozen or so years to give birth to Isaac. Get your fire back, get your dreams back. You are still going to give birth to everything that God has placed in your heart.

This is what Caleb did. He and Joshua were two of the twelve men whom Moses sent in to spy out the Promised Land. They came back and said, "We are well able to take the land; let us go in at once." They knew the promise was in them, but the other ten spies' negative report convinced the entire nation of Israel, camped next door to the Promised Land, that they could not defeat their enemies, and they never did enter the Promised Land.

Forty years later, when Caleb was eighty-five years old, he could have been sitting in a rocking chair, taking it easy. But Caleb was still fired up about not making it into the Promised Land. He knew the promise was still in him. He went back to the place he'd been forty years earlier, the place where the others would not go, and he declared, "Give me this mountain." What's interesting is that this mountain had three fierce giants living on it—the giants the other ten spies said made them feel like grasshoppers. It would have been a lot easier to ask for a mountain with less opposition—maybe just one giant, or better yet, none. But Caleb's attitude was, *God, this is what You promised me, and I'm not going to settle for mediocrity when I know You put greatness in me. Yes, I'm older; yes, it's been a long time. I've made mistakes. I've gone through disappointments. But God, I still believe the promise is in me.* At eighty-five years old, he went in, conquered the enemies, drove out the giants, took the mountain, and saw the dream come to pass.

You may think it's been too long. You're too old. You've missed too many opportunities. God is saying, "You can still make it into your promised land. You can still do something great." The Scripture tells us to fan the flame, to stir up the gifts, for the promise is in you.

> *Fan the flame, stir up the gifts, for the promise is in you.*

Don't Be Surprised by Opposition

My brother, Paul, is a surgeon and spends several months a year in Africa performing operations in small villages. One of the safari guides told him that when a gazelle or a wildebeest is pregnant and about to give birth, a lion will closely stalk that animal. Day after day, the lion will follow the pregnant mother, waiting for her to go into labor. The lion knows that when she goes into labor, she's an easy target, because she can't defend herself. So the lion will actually wait for the mother to go into labor and then not only attack and kill her, but the baby as well.

It's the same principle in life. You will face your greatest attacks when you're about to give birth to the dreams God placed in your heart. The enemy waits until you're close to the promotion, close to the breakthrough. He'll strike when you're just about to step up to a new level. Don't be surprised if you face opposition or you go through a disappointment. Perhaps a friend whom you were counting on is not there. Or it's taking longer than you expected. That simply means you're about to give birth to what God has placed in your heart. The good news is the forces that are for you are greater than the forces that are against you. Your destiny cannot be stopped by a bad break, by disappointments, by opposition, or by other people. God has the final say. He says, "No weapon formed against you will ever prosper."

You may be facing big challenges, things are coming against you. That's a sign you're about to see a dream come to pass. Now is not the time to get discouraged. Now is the time to dig your heels in and declare, "I am in it to win it. I know the promise is in me. I'm not going to let this disappointment, this setback, or this person steal my destiny. I'm going to give birth to everything that God has placed in my heart."

That was the attitude of a young man

named Troy. He came from a single-parent home. His family had been through so many struggles. His mother became ill and had to have brain surgery. During a huge flood, they lost everything. It was one bad break after another. It didn't look as though Troy would ever get the opportunity to do anything great. The odds were against him. But Troy always had a big dream for his life. When he was in the third grade, he wrote in a school paper that he was going to get a scholarship to go to college. Even as a young boy, he could feel the promise in him to go further, to leave his mark. His dream was to go to Georgetown University, to get a doctorate in international relations, and to become secretary of state of the United States.

For Troy's single-parent mother, that level of education seemed impossible. Troy could have thought, *Too bad for me. I've got a big dream, but I don't have the money. I don't have the connections.* But Troy's attitude was, *The promise is in me. What God has spoken over my life will come to pass.* Those are the better thoughts he needed. He didn't sit back and expect God to do it all for him. He excelled in school. He took college courses in the tenth grade. He graduated number two in his high school class. Troy received not just one scholarship; he was awarded nine scholarships that were worth over one million dollars. His bachelor's degree, his master's, and his doctoral studies are totally paid for at Georgetown University.

What God has promised you, He will bring to pass. You may not see a way, but God has a way. If you'll be the best that you can be, right where you are, God will get you to where He wants you to be.

A Fire Shut Up in Your Bones

In the Scripture, God put a promise in Jeremiah that he would be a prophet and speak to the nations. Jeremiah was young, afraid, and he didn't think he could do it. People and obstacles came against him. He got so discouraged that he was about to give up. Eventually, Jeremiah began to tell God how bad it was. He listed one complaint after another. "God, these people are mocking me. When I speak, they make fun of me. I'm being ridiculed. I'm tired. I'm lonely. I'm intimidated." Jeremiah had a long list.

But just when you thought Jeremiah was going to quit, he said, "God, I feel like giving up, but Your word in my heart is like fire shut up in my bones." He was saying, "God, I don't see how it can happen. All the odds are against me. But this promise You put in me will not go away. It's like fire. It's like a burning. I can't get away from it." When Jeremiah began to think better and let the fire burn, his life passion was restored.

You may be at a place where you can easily be discouraged and give up on what God has placed in your heart. But the good news is, as was true for Jeremiah, there is a fire shut up in your bones. There is a promise that God has spoken over you that will not die. You can try to ignore it, and your mind or others will try to convince you it's never going to happen. But deep down, you'll feel a burning, a restlessness, a fire. That's the promise God put in you. God loves you too much to let you remain average. He's going to push you into greatness. You're going to accomplish more than you thought possible. You're going to go further than you dreamed. You're going to see the exceeding greatness of God's power. What He's spoken over your life will come to pass.

You don't need anyone else to give birth to what God has placed in your heart. Quit looking for the other person. You are the right person. You are equipped. You are anointed. You have what it takes. Now stir up

> *You're going to accomplish more than you thought possible.*

what's on the inside. It's time for you to be celebrated. It's time for you to rise to a new level. It's time for you to do something great!

CHAPTER SEVEN

Ask Big

When God laid out the plan for your life, He didn't just put into it what you need to get by to survive, to endure until the end. He put more than enough in it. He's a God of abundance. We see this all through the Scripture. After Jesus multiplied the little boy's lunch of five loaves of bread and two fish, thousands of people ate, and yet there were twelve basketfuls of leftovers. It is interesting that they had counted the people beforehand, so Jesus knew how many people were in the crowd that day. If He had wanted to be exact, He could have made just enough so there would be no leftovers.

On purpose, He made more than enough. That's the God we serve.

David said, "My cup runs over." He had an abundance, more than he needed. Yes, we should thank God that our needs are supplied. We should be grateful that we have enough, but don't settle there. That's not your destiny. He is a more-than-enough God. He wants you to have an abundance, so you can be a blessing to those around you.

This is where the Israelites missed it. They had been in slavery for so many years that they became conditioned to not having enough, to barely getting by. When Pharaoh got upset with Moses, he told his foremen to have the Israelites make the same amount of bricks without the hay and straw being provided for them. I'm sure the Israelites prayed, "God, please, help us to make our quotas. God, please, help us to find the supplies that we need." They prayed from a slave mentality, from a limited mind-set. Instead of asking to be freed from their oppressors, they were asking to become better slaves. Instead of praying for what God promised them, the land flowing with milk and honey, they prayed that God would help them function better in their dysfunction.

Are you asking today to become a better slave or are you asking for the abundant, overflowing, more-than-enough life that God has for you? God says you are to reign in life, that you are blessed and you cannot be cursed, that whatever you touch will prosper and succeed. Don't pray to just get by, to endure. Dare to ask big. Ask for what God promised you. The medical report may not look good. That's okay. There's another report: "God, You said You would restore health back to me. You said the number of my days, You will fulfill." Maybe you've gone through a disappointment, a bad break. Don't pray, "God, help me to deal with this loneliness. God, help me to put up with this depression." That's a slave mentality. Turn it around with some better thoughts: "God, You said you would give me beauty for these ashes, joy for this mourning, and that You would pay me back double for this unfair situation." Or your dream may look impossible. You don't see how it can work out: "God, You said Your blessings would chase me down, that I'm surrounded by favor, that goodness and mercy are following me, and that you would give me the desires of my heart."

Take the limits off God and ask big, not from a slave mentality, not from a limited mind-set. Don't ask God to help you function better in your dysfunction. Ask God to help you think bigger and better so you can live better. Ask Him for your dreams. Ask Him for new levels. Ask Him for explosive blessings. Ask Him to propel you into your purpose.

> *Don't pray to just get by, to endure. Dare to ask big.*

More Than Enough

This is what a lady I know did. She has four small grandchildren whom she ended up having to raise. She wasn't planning on it, but something happened with her daughter. At first, she was a little discouraged, not knowing how it was going to work out. Three of the children were in private school, which was very expensive, and the grandmother didn't have the extra funds to keep paying their tuition. She could've prayed from a slave mentality: "God, this isn't fair. I'll never be able to provide for my grandchildren. Please just help us to survive." Instead, she had the boldness to ask big. She said, "God, I don't have the funds to keep my grandchildren in private school, but I know You own it all. You're a God of abundance. And, God, I'm asking You to make a way, even though I don't see how it can ever happen."

At the end of the children's first school year, she owed a small amount on tuition, so she went to the school to pay. The secretary called up her records on the computer and said, "No, you don't owe anything. Everything's all paid up."

"That can't be," the grandmother responded.

"I have the notice right here. This says that I owe this amount."

The secretary turned the monitor around and said, "No, ma'am. It says right here that all three of the children's tuitions have been paid, not only for the rest of this year, but all the way through the eighth grade." An anonymous donor had stepped up and pre-paid it for years to come!

God can make things happen that you could never make happen. He's already placed abundance in your future. He's already lined up the right people, the breaks you need, doors to open that you could never open. My question is, "Are you asking big?" Or are you letting your circumstances—how you were raised, what somebody said—talk you out of it? If you go through life praying only "barely getting by" prayers, you'll miss the fullness of your destiny.

But when you get this in your spirit, that the God who breathed life into you, the God who called you, set you apart, and crowned you with favor, is a more-than-enough God, an abundant God, an overflowing God, you'll have a boldness to ask for big things. Those are power thoughts that will change

> *If you go through life praying only "barely getting by" prayers, you'll miss the fullness of your destiny.*

how you live. You won't ask to just manage the addiction, but to be free from the addiction. You won't ask to just pay your bills, but to be totally out of debt, so you can be a blessing to others. You won't ask to just see your child get back on the right course, but that God will use him to make his mark on this generation.

What Is It That You Want?

The book of Matthew records the story of Jesus walking through a town where there were two blind men by the side of the road. When they heard all the commotion and that Jesus was passing by, they started shouting,

"Jesus, have mercy on us!" Jesus walked over to them and said, "What is it that you want me to do for you?" It seemed like a strange question. It's obvious what they needed. They were blind. Why did Jesus ask them? Because He wanted to see what they were believing. They could've said, "Jesus, we just need some help out here. We're blind. We just need a little better place to live or some cash for some food." If they had asked from a limited mentality, it would have kept them in defeat. Instead, they asked big. They said, "Lord, we want to see. We want our eyes to be opened." They were saying, "We know you can do the impossible." When Jesus heard their request, He touched their eyes, and instantly they could see.

God is asking us the same thing he asked those two blind men: "What is it that you want Me to do for you?" Now, how you answer is going to have a great impact on what God does. Don't say, "God, I just want to make it through this year. Have you seen what apartments are renting for these days?"

"God, my family's so dysfunctional, just help us to survive." "God, I don't like my job. Just help me to endure it." That is going to limit your destiny.

Do what those blind men did. Dare to ask big. "God, I want to be free from this addiction." "God, I want to meet the right person." "God, I want to see my whole family serve you." "God, I want to start my own business." Ask for your dreams. Ask even for things that seem impossible. The Scripture says, "You ask and do not receive, because you ask amiss." That word *amiss* in the original language means "sick, weak, miserable."

When we ask to become better slaves, that's a sick prayer. When we ask to get by, to endure, to barely make it, that's a weak prayer. That's asking amiss. God is saying, "I created the whole universe. I own it all. Don't come to Me with a sick prayer, a weak prayer, asking Me to help you live in mediocrity, endure the trouble, and survive another month. When you come to Me, ask big, knowing that I'm a God of more than enough." He's saying, "Ask Me to show out in your life. Ask Me to heal you from that disease. Ask Me to accelerate your goals."

When you ask big, God calls that a healthy prayer. That's when He says to the angels, "Go to work. Release My favor. Loose those chains. Open up new doors." "Well, Joel, I'm just praying that I'll make it through these tough times. Business is really slow." May I say this respectfully? That's a sick prayer. That prayer has the flu! "I'm just praying that I'll learn how to manage this addiction. Grandmother had it. Mother had it. Now I do, too." That's a weak prayer. Your attitude should be, *God, this addiction keeps getting passed down through my family line, but I believe this is a new day and that You've raised me up to put a stop to it—that I will be the one to break the generational curse and start the generational blessing.*

Don't ask to become a better slave. Ask to be the difference maker. Ask to set a new standard. When you say, "God, help me to get that scholarship so I can go to college," that's not just being hopeful, just being positive. That's your faith being released. That's what allows

God to do great things. Or, "God, I don't have the funds for the building project just yet, but, Lord, I want to thank You that opportunity is headed my way, that blessings are chasing me down." No more sick prayers. Take the limits off God. Ask big. This is the year for God to show out in your life, to accelerate His goodness, to propel you into your destiny.

No More Weak, Sick Prayers

This is what a man by the name of Jabez did in the Scripture. His name literally means "pain, sorrow, suffering." Every time someone said, "Hello, Jabez," they were saying "Hello, trouble." "Hello, sorrow." "Hello, pain." They were prophesying defeat and failure. You can imagine how he could have let that keep him in mediocrity, make him feel inferior and insecure. There was something different about Jabez, though. Despite his rough upbringing, despite what people labeled him, he looked up to the heavens and said, "God, I'm asking you to bless me indeed." He could have just said, "God, bless me." That would've been okay. But he had the boldness to ask big.

Jabez was a man who was supposed to have trouble and heartache, to live depressed and defeated, but he shook off the slave mentality. His attitude was, *It doesn't matter what people say about me. It doesn't matter what my circumstances look like. I know who I am—a child of the Most High God.* He went on to say, "God, enlarge my territories." He was saying, "God, help me to go beyond the norm. Let me see abundance. Let me see more of Your favor." I'm sure thoughts told him, "Jabez, God's not going to bless you. You come from the wrong family. Your own parents labeled you 'sorrow, pain, trouble.'" But people don't determine your destiny; God does. The Scripture says that God granted Jabez his request. God blessed him indeed.

Like Jabez, you may have plenty of reasons to settle where you are—what you didn't get, what people said, how impossible it looks. The odds may be against you, but the good news is that God is for you. He is more powerful than any force that's trying to stop you. He knows how to make up for what you didn't get. He can thrust you further than you ever imagined, but you have to do as Jabez did and pray bold prayers. Ask in spite of what the circumstances look like. Ask in spite of what people are telling you. Ask in spite of what the enemy keeps whispering in your ear.

Jabez could have prayed a weak, sick prayer and thought, *God, I've had some bad breaks. I had a rough upbringing. I'm just asking You to help me survive.* If he had done that, we wouldn't be talking about him today. If you're going to beat the odds, stand out in the crowd, and reach your highest potential, you have to learn this principle of asking big.

Today Is Your Birthday

God said in Psalm 2, from *The Message* translation, "You're my son, and today is your birthday. What do you want? Name it: Nations as a present? Continents as a prize? You can command them all to dance for you." Notice how big God thinks. Sometimes we're praying for a three dollar-an-hour raise; God's talking about giving you nations. We're praying for a promotion; God's got a business for you to own. We're praying to pay our bills; God's planning on blessing you so you can pay other people's bills. We're looking at the five loaves and two fish; God's thinking about the twelve basketfuls of leftovers.

What does that mean, "Today is

What do you want?

Nations as a present?

your birthday"? On your birthday, more than at any other time, you feel entitled to ask for something out of the ordinary. Normally, you don't want anybody to go out of the way for you, but on your birthday, you think, *Okay, I'm going to ask for that favor. I'm going to ask for a new outfit or for a set of golf clubs.* Over time, as we get older, our enthusiasm may go down a little, but think back to when you were a child. You knew that was your special day. You had the boldness to ask for what you really wanted.

A while ago, a little boy came up to me out in the hallway. He's five years old, and I see him at the church all the time. He came running up, so excited, and exclaimed, "It's my birthday today!" I gave him a big hug and told him, "Happy birthday!" I walked about five steps away, and he came back and grabbed my leg and said it again: "It's my birthday!" I thought, *I know, you just told me five seconds ago.* We hugged and did it all again as though it was the first time. This happened again and again and again. I could hardly get through the hallway. About the seventh time, he came up and grabbed my leg. This time, instead of telling me it was his birthday, he looked up and said, "What are you going to get me for my birthday?" The reason he kept coming back is because he felt entitled to a present. He knew it was his special day.

God is saying, "When you pray, act as though it's your birthday. Come to Me with a boldness. Ask Me for what you really want. Don't be shy. Don't hold back. Tell Me your dreams. Tell Me what you're believing for. Ask for the secret things I placed in your heart."

When our son, Jonathan, was a little boy, he liked the little action figures of the Power Rangers. He never asked for that much, but on his sixth birthday, he said, "Dad, I really want that new Power Ranger I saw on television." We drove to the closest toy store, but they were sold out of that Power Ranger. We drove to another store, and they didn't have it—and another, and another, and another. Normally, I would've given up, but it was my son's birthday. I didn't want to disappoint him. Finally, we found one at a toy store an hour away. It took half the day to get this little fourteen-dollar action figure. But as a father, I didn't mind going out of my way.

You know how, as parents, you'll do anything for your children, especially on their birthday. How much more will your Heavenly Father make things happen for you? Ask Him for your dreams. Ask Him to turn your child around. Ask Him for your healing. You're not inconveniencing God. "Well, Joel, God has bigger things to deal with than me." No, you are God's biggest deal. You're the apple of His eye. You're His most prized possession. Just like I ran all over the city to find that action figure to give my son what he was dreaming for on his birthday, God will move heaven and earth to bring about His destiny in your life. Dare to ask big.

It Is Your Father's Good Pleasure

Too often, instead of approaching God as though it's our birthday, believing that He'll do something special, we do just the opposite. "Joel, I can't ask for what I really want. That wouldn't be right. That would be greedy. That would be selfish." The Scripture says it is the Father's good pleasure to give you the kingdom. Nothing makes God happier than for Him to see you step up to who you were created to be. Psalm 2 says, "Today is your birthday. What do you want?" Notice, today is always in the present. When you get up tomorrow morning, God is saying, "Today is your birthday." Two weeks from now, "Today is your birthday." Seven years from now, "Today is your birthday." Every morning when you get up, just imagine God saying, "Happy birthday, Son." "Happy birthday, Daughter." Why does He do this? So you'll have the boldness to ask for things that you wouldn't normally ask for.

When I received word that the Compaq

Center was coming available, something ignited on the inside of me. I knew it was supposed to be ours, but every voice said,

"Today is your birthday. What do you want?" Notice, today is always in the present.

"It's never going to happen. It's too big, Joel. You don't deserve it. Who do you think you are to even ask for it?" Instead of believing those lies, I did what I'm asking you to do. I went to God as though it was my birthday, and I said, "God, I know this is far out. Normally, I'd never ask for it, but, God, I believe You put this in our path. This is part of my destiny. So, God, I'm asking You to make a way, even though I don't see a way."

What is interesting is that in all the big things I've ever asked God for, I've never once felt as though He said, "Joel, you've got a lot of nerve. What are you doing, asking for that?" Just the opposite. In my heart, I can feel God whispering, "Joel, I love the fact that you dare to ask big. I love the fact that you believe I can do the impossible." Of course, everything I've asked for hasn't come to pass, but the point is, if you go to God with childlike faith, believing that it's your birthday, asking for things that you wouldn't normally ask for, there will be times when you see God show out in your life in ways greater than you ever imagined.

Stand Out and Make a Difference

This is what Solomon did. In Psalm 72, he prayed what seemed to be a very self-centered prayer. He asked God to make him well-known, that his fame would spread throughout the land, that the wealth and honor of other nations would be brought to him, and that kings and queens would bow down before him. You would think God would say, "Solomon, what's wrong with you? I'm not going to make you famous. I'm not going to give you this honor, wealth, and influence. You need to learn some humility." But God didn't rebuke him. God didn't tell him he was selfish and greedy. God did exactly what he asked for. Solomon became one of the most famous people of his day. The queen of Sheba came, bowed down before him, and brought him gold and silver.

Here's the key: The reason God answered that bold prayer is because Solomon went on to pray, "God, if You'll make my name famous, if You'll give me influence and wealth, I will use it to help the widows, to take care of the orphans, to bring justice to the oppressed, to give a voice to those who don't have any voice." He asked big, not just so he would look impressive, drive the fanciest chariot, and live in the biggest palace. It was so he could lift the fallen, restore the broken, and help the hurting to advance God's kingdom. God has no problem giving you influence, honor, wealth, and even fame, as long as your dream, in some way, is connected to helping others, to making this world a better place. When your thoughts align with God's thoughts for others, He will help make your life better.

Ask big so you can lift the fallen, restore the broken, and help the hurting to advance the kingdom.

God is raising up a new generation of Solomons, people who have the boldness to say, "God, make me famous in my field. Let my gifts and talents stand out. Let my work be so excellent, so inspiring, that people all around me know who I am, not for my glory, but so I can use my influence to advance Your kingdom." Whatever field you're in—medicine, sales, construction, accounting, teaching—I dare you to pray, "God, make me famous in my field. Let me shine. Give me influence."

If you're an architect, dare to pray, "God, give me ideas, creativity, and designs that stand out." Then use your influence to design a boys' home or an orphanage.

If you're a mechanic, dare to pray, "God, make me famous. Let me be so skilled and have so much expertise that people come to me to see how it's done." Then use your influence to fix the cars of single moms, to mentor young men and teach them how to do it.

If you're in the medical profession, dare to pray, "God, make me famous. Let me develop procedures that benefit mankind." Then use that influence to help those who can't afford it. There's no limit to what God will do for you if you'll use what He's given you to help others.

One time, I was playing basketball with some friends, and I had to leave early to go to a doctor's appointment. A teammate of mine works in the medical field, and he asked me who I was going to see. I said, "Dr. Price, a friend of mine."

He looked up and said, "*The* Dr. Price?"

"No, *just* Dr. Price," I replied. "I've known him for thirty years."

"Is he *the* Dr. Price who's in infectious medicine?"

"Yes, that's him," I said.

"Oh, man," he exclaimed, "he's the best! He's famous. People come to see him from all over."

I mentioned earlier what Dr. Price does with

his "fame," his wealth, and his influence—he uses it to help needy people in third-world countries. Dr. Price never dreamed he would be where he is today. God made him famous— not TMZ famous, but famous in his field.

I wonder what would happen if you would dare to pray, "God, make me famous. God, cause me to stand out so I can make a big difference in this world." God can make things happen that you could never make happen. He'll cause you to stand out so you can use your influence, not only to reach your goals, but so you can help others along the way.

Now, do your part. No more sick prayers. No more weak prayers. Get rid of that slave mentality. Go to God as though it's your birthday. Ask Him for your dreams. As Jabez did, dare to say, "God, bless me indeed." If you'll do this, I believe and declare, as He did for Solomon, God is going to give you more influence, more resources, and more notoriety. You're going to accomplish your dreams, rise higher than you ever thought possible, and become everything God created you to be.

CHAPTER EIGHT

You Have What You Need

So often we think, *If I had more money, I could accomplish my dreams. If I had a bigger house, I'd be happy. If I had more talent, a better personality, and if I knew the right people, I could do something great.* But as long as you feel as though you're lacking, you don't have enough, and you were shortchanged, you'll make excuses to be less than your best.

You have to get a new perspective. God has given you exactly what you need for the season you're in. You have the talent, the friends, the connections, the resources, and the experience you need for right now. It doesn't mean that's all you're ever going to have. You may need more next month or next year. When that time comes, God will make sure that you have more then.

Psalm 34 says, "Those who trust in the Lord will never lack any good thing." Because your trust is in the Lord, you don't have to worry. Whatever you need, God will make sure you have it when you need it. You won't lack any good thing. This means that if you don't have it right now, don't fight it. Don't be discouraged. You don't need it right now. Our attitude should be, *I'm equipped, empowered, and anointed for this moment. I am not lacking, shortchanged, inadequate, missing out, or less than. I have what I need for today.*

This approach is so much better than thinking, *If I just had the finances...If the loan would have gone through...If she would have been my friend...If I had a better personality...* If you needed a better personality, God would have given you a better personality. God wasn't having a bad day when He created you. If you needed more talent, God would have given you more talent. If

you needed more
friends, you would
have more friends.
Take what you have

> *Take what you have and make the most of it.*

and make the most of it. It's what you need
for right now.

You Are Lacking Nothing

Years ago I used to think, *If we had a bigger building...If we had more members...If I could minister better...If I had more experience...* There was always something I didn't have or I couldn't do, always some reason I couldn't feel good about myself. If I hadn't changed those thoughts, they would have put limits on how I lived.

One day I realized what I'm telling you: I have what I need for the season I'm in right now. I have the strength that I need for today. It may not be enough strength for tomorrow, but that's okay. When tomorrow comes, God will give me strength for that day. I have the talent, the qualifications, and the experience I need for right now. It may not be as much as somebody else has, but that's okay. I'm not competing with them. I'm competing with myself to become the best me that I can possibly be.

Several years ago, someone published an article that talked about how I haven't been to seminary and how I wasn't qualified to lead a large ministry. At first that bothered me. Then I read Galatians 1, where the apostle Paul, who wrote about half the books of the New Testament, said, "I was not appointed by any group or by human authority...my call came from God who raised Jesus from the dead."

People may not approve you. Don't worry about it. God approves you. People didn't call you. People don't determine your destiny. People can't stop God's plan for your life. God called you. God equipped you. God anointed you. When you come to the end of your life, you don't have to answer to people. You'll answer to Almighty God. Don't let what some person says or does make you feel less than or unqualified. You've been hand-picked by the Creator of the universe. You are lacking nothing for the season that you're in right now. Now quit thinking about all the things that you don't have and all the things that you wish were different.

"But, Joel, all I have is this old car. I'm depressed." Have a new attitude and say, "This old car is all I need right now. God is on the throne directing my steps. When I need more, He will give me more."

"All I have is this one friend." Turn it around. "This one friend is all I need for this season. I'm not going to sit around in self-pity. When I need more friends, God will give me more friends."

"All I have is this low-level job." Tell yourself, "That's all I need right now. When it's my time to be promoted, nothing can stand against my God. I will be promoted. But in the meantime, I'm going to keep being my best right where I am."

This is an empowering way to live. You're

not making excuses. You're not feeling short-changed. You're thinking better, so you'll live better.

"If I just had more money..." If you needed more money to fulfill your destiny right now and God withheld it, He wouldn't be a just God. The truth is, God has already lined up the right people, the right opportunities, the finances, the wisdom, the good breaks, and the protection you need. It's in your future. As long as you keep honoring God, He will give you what you need when you need it. That means if you don't have it right now, you don't need it right now. My question is, "Will you trust Him?" Will you keep a good attitude and be your best, even though it's taking longer than you expected, even though the problem hasn't turned around, and even though a dream hasn't come to pass? If you will be faithful where you are now, knowing that you have exactly what you need for the season that you're in, God will get you to where you're supposed to be.

Much, Much More

In the book of 2 Samuel is the story of how King David got off course with his life. The prophet Nathan was correcting him. In doing so, he reminded David of what God had brought him through. David had experienced God's goodness, favor, protection, provision, and healing down through the years. God made an interesting statement through Nathan: "David, if it had not been enough, I would have given you much, much more." In other words, "David, looking back over your life, if you were ever lacking, if you ever needed more wisdom, more favor, more protection, or more finance, God would have given it to you."

That tells me that what I have right now is what I need to fulfill my destiny. The moment it becomes insufficient is the moment God will give me more. The moment something starts to keep you from your destiny, the moment it begins to stop God's plan for your life, is the moment God will show up, the moment He will intervene. So if it hasn't happened yet, don't be discouraged, thinking that it's never going to work out. If it hasn't happened, you haven't needed it. When you need it, it won't be one second late. The moment you need a new friend, the moment you need a good break, the moment you need an idea, it will show up. God is closely watching your life. You are His most prized possession. He is saying to you what He said to David: "If it's ever not enough, you can count on Me. I will always be there to give you more."

In 1959, my father was the pastor of a large denominational church. They had nearly a thousand members and had just built a beautiful new sanctuary. Back then, that was a big deal. My father's future looked very bright. But through a series of events, the day came

> *What you have right now is what you need to fulfill your destiny.*

when he knew he was supposed to leave that church and start Lakewood. It didn't make sense from a practical standpoint. He didn't have a building or any organization backing him up. Most of his friends thought he was making a mistake and didn't support him. He could have made a list of all the things he didn't have. If he had stayed focused on that, he would never have moved off dead center.

But my father took a step of faith and started Lakewood with ninety people in an old, run-down feed store. Instead of thinking, *All I have are these ninety people*, his attitude was, *These ninety people are all I need*. Instead of thinking, *All I have is this old feed store*, his better thought was, *This old feed store is all I need*. When you realize the Creator of the universe is directing your steps, giving you what you need, and that the moment it becomes inadequate, He promises to show up and give you more, you won't go around discouraged, thinking, *This is not fair. Why don't I get any good breaks? When is this ever going to change?* You'll just keep being your best, honoring God.

That's what my father did and today, over fifty-seven years later, Lakewood is still going strong. Maybe you're discouraged because of what has not happened in your life. You're wondering when the situation is going to turn around, when you're going to get that good break. Quit being stressed over it. God has you in the palm of His hands. He has written every day of your life in His book. God knows what you need and when you need it, and He knows how to get it to you. If you don't have something right now, you didn't miss it. You didn't get shortchanged. God didn't forget about you. As long as you're honoring Him, at the right time, when you need them, the right people will show up. When you need it, the finance will come. When you need it, the healing, the restoration, and the vindication will find you. If it hasn't happened yet, don't sit around being sour. Have the attitude, *I don't need it. When I need it, God promises it won't be one second late.*

Do Not Despise Small Beginnings

The Scripture tells the story of how Jesus met a Samaritan woman at a well and asked her for something to drink. She was a little surprised because in those days the Jews didn't have anything to do with the Samaritans, let alone a Jewish man speaking with a Samaritan woman. She said, "How can You ask me for something to drink?"

Jesus said, "If you knew who I am, you would ask of Me and I would give you living water."

She immediately began to view the circumstances from a human perspective. She said, "But, sir, You don't have anything to draw water with. You don't have a bucket or a pail. How can You give me living water?"

I wonder how many times we do the same thing. God tells us He is going to do something great in our lives. Down deep, He puts a dream on the inside that we're going to rise higher. We're going to see our marriage restored. We're going to get healthy again. We feel it strongly, but as the Samaritan woman did, we start looking at what we don't have, the way we were raised, the obstacles in our path. Before long, we talk ourselves out of it. "I can't do anything great. I don't have the talent. My marriage is too far gone. The medical report is too bad." You're just looking with a limited natural perspective, but we serve a supernatural God. He can take something that is ordinary, breathe on it, and turn it into something that's extraordinary. You may have average talent, but when God breathes on your life, you will go further than people who have great talent. Don't talk yourself out of it.

All David had was a slingshot and five smooth stones. It looked insignificant, ordinary, certainly nothing special. But God breathed on him, and he defeated Goliath and became the king of Israel. Samson was surrounded by a huge army. Everywhere he looked there were horses, chariots, and weapons. All he had was the jawbone of a donkey.

No weapon. No armor. Nobody backing him up. But he picked up that jawbone, God breathed on him, and he defeated an entire army of a thousand men. All Moses had was an ordinary stick, something he found on the ground, yet when he picked up that rod and held it in the air, the Red Sea supernaturally parted. All my father had was ninety people and an abandoned, run-down feed store, yet God breathed on them and did something extraordinary.

Don't underestimate what you have. It may look small and insignificant. Compared to what you're facing, perhaps it seems utterly useless. All the odds are against you. But when God breathes on your life, the odds dramatically change. You and

All Moses had was an ordinary stick, but consider what he did with it.

God are a majority. God can open doors that should have never opened in the natural. God can take you beyond where your talent and your education say you should be.

God can make a way even when you don't see a way. It's not enough just to have faith in God. That's important, but you have to have faith in what God has given you. You are not lacking. You were not shortchanged. You are not at a disadvantage. The Creator of the universe is breathing on your life. He is breathing on your health, breathing on your finances, breathing on your marriage. If you will be confident in what God has given you, He can take what looks like little and turn it into much.

The Scripture even says, "Don't despise the day of small beginnings." In other words, don't look at what you have and say, "I can't do anything great. I don't have a lot of talent." "A feed store? God, I need a big building." "A low-level job? God, I wanted to be in management." What God has given you right now may seem small, but don't let that fool you. When you use what you

Don't underestimate what you have.

have, God will multiply it. You will see an explosion of His goodness.

Use What You've Been Given

On one occasion, Jesus had been teaching thousands of people. It was getting late in the day and everyone was hungry. Jesus turned to His disciples and said, "I want you to feed all these people." They didn't have any food out there in the wilderness. There were no grocery stores. On the surface, it seemed as though what Jesus asked was impossible. But here's the key: God will never ask you to do something and then not give you the ability to do it. "I can't raise this child. He's too difficult." God wouldn't have given you the child if you weren't able to raise him. "The people at work are driving me crazy." When God gave you that job, He gave you the ability to be there with a good attitude. "I can't accomplish my dreams. I don't know

the right people." The moment God put the
dream in your heart, He lined up everything
you need to bring it to pass.

The disciples said to Jesus, "We can't feed
all these people. It's impossible. We don't have
any food. Send them away so they can go
to the villages and buy food for themselves."

Jesus listened to all their excuses, and
finally He said to them, "You've told Me
all about what you don't have. All I want
to know is what you do have."

They said, "We just have five loaves of
bread and two small fish. But what is this
among so many?" They had considered it
and dismissed it. It was not enough.

"Joel, I believe I could do something great
if I had more going for me, if I had more talent, more friends, and more money." Get rid
of the "I don't have enough" mentality. God
controls the whole universe. That's the better
thought you need. He is saying to you today
what Jesus said to the disciples: "Give Me
what you have. Don't make excuses. Don't
sit on the sidelines of life feeling intimidated

and shortchanged. Put your life, your goals, and your dreams into My hands."

Jesus took the five loaves and the two fish, prayed over them, and they supernaturally multiplied. That small meal ended up feeding probably fifteen thousand people, plus there were basketfuls of leftovers to take home. That's what happens when you give God what you have. He will multiply it. Are you talking yourself out of something God has put in your heart?

I read a story about a young lady by the name of Mary Bethune. She was born in South Carolina in 1875, the fifteenth of seventeen children. Her parents were former slaves. Despite the odds being against her, she was able to get a good education and even went to college. From the time she was a little girl, her dream was always to teach young people. She was a straight-A student. You couldn't meet a finer young woman. She graduated from college and turned her application in to become a missionary in Africa. Several months later, she got a notification that she had been turned down. For some reason, she wasn't accepted. But instead of sitting around thinking about how badly life was treating her, she had the attitude, *I didn't get that position. I must not have needed it. If it was going to keep me from my destiny, God would have never allowed it.*

Eventually Mary Bethune decided to start her own school. She didn't have any money, or a building, or any supplies or equipment. She found some old cardboard boxes and used them for desks. She would take red berries each day and drain the juice out of them, so her students could use that for ink in their pens. A few years later, a local college noticed what was happening and asked her to join forces with them in what became known as the Bethune-Cookman College. In 1936, President Franklin Roosevelt appointed her as the director of the Division of Negro Affairs and an advisor to his cabinet on black employment, education, and civil rights issues, making her the first African-American woman ever to become a presidential advisor.

What am I saying? What you have may seem small, but don't dismiss it. If you'll use what God has given you, He will multiply it. He will not only bring your dreams to pass, but He will do more than you can ask or think.

The Sound of Footsteps

The Scripture tells of four lepers who were so desperate for food, they were marching toward the enemy's camp. These four men had nothing: no supplies, no food, no protection, not even their health. In the natural, they didn't have a chance of surviving. They could have been sitting around depressed, focused on what they didn't have. Instead they were using what they did have. As they were marching toward the enemy's camp, God multiplied the sound of their footsteps. It sounded like a huge army was attacking. Their enemies took off running for their lives and left all their supplies behind, saving not only the lepers' lives but the people of Samaria as well.

"Well, Joel, I don't have a lot of talent." Maybe not. But do you have any footsteps? "I don't have a lot of money." Maybe not. But do you have any red berries? "I don't have a big building for my new business." Maybe not. But do you have an old, run-down feed store? If you'll use what God has given you, He will multiply it. He will multiply your talent, multiply your resources, and multiply your influence. God is not into addition. He is into multiplication. What you have today may seem small, but if you'll keep honoring God, it's not going to stay small. You're going to come into supernatural increase, good breaks, divine connections, and opportunities that you've never seen before. You have exactly what you need to fulfill your destiny. Now here's the key: You may not have as much as a family member, a coworker, or a friend. But that's okay. You're not running their race. You're running your race. If God gave you what they have, it wouldn't help you. It would hinder you. You're not anointed to be them. You're anointed to be you.

When David went out to face Goliath, King Saul tried to get David to wear his armor. David didn't have any protection, and his only weapon was his slingshot. Saul had good intentions. He said, "David, at least wear my armor. You're going to go out there and get killed." However, David was much smaller than King Saul, and when he put that armor on, it swallowed him. It didn't help him. It weighed him down. That's because what God has given other people is not going to work for you. Don't try to be like somebody else. "I wish I had their talent, their looks, their personality." If you put that armor on, you would be uncomfortable, just as David was. It would slow you down. Why? It wasn't designed for you. You are unique. You are one of a kind. God custom-made your armor. You are wearing designer armor. Nobody has what you have. When you go

> *You are wearing designer armor. Nobody has what you have.*

out today, you need to walk with some swag!

David took that armor off and said, "No, thanks. This is not for me. I can't be who God created me to be wearing somebody else's armor. I have what I need." It may not be as much as somebody else has—you may have less talent, less resources, and fewer friends—but if you'll walk in your own anointing, if you'll use what God has given you, you will go further than people who have more talent and more resources, because God is breathing on your life. That's what happened with David. He defeated Goliath with less equipment. Goliath was wearing a full set of armor and had a huge spear. All David had was the slingshot. The difference was that the slingshot was a part of David's divine destiny. If he had looked at it and thought, *It's nothing. It's small. It's insignificant. I can't do this*, he would have missed his destiny.

Don't dismiss what God has given you. It may not seem as impressive as what somebody else has. You may not have the talent, the looks, the personality, the income, or the influence that they have. But consider that what God has given you has been custom-made for you alone. He specifically gave you your gifts, your talents, your looks, and your personality. It wasn't a random happening. God didn't close His eyes and say, "Here, just take this. It will do." No, God matched you for your world. He put in you exactly what you need to fulfill His plan for your life.

Be Confident in Who You Are

A few years ago I was speaking to several hundred pastors. Afterward we had a time for questions. One pastor that stood up was a very large man, about six feet five inches tall and three hundred pounds. I am five feet nine inches tall. Television makes you look bigger than you really are. They were surprised by how small I am. He said very dramatically, "Joel, I just want to know, how much do you weigh?" I smiled and said, "I'm one hundred and fifty pounds of pure steel!"

You have to be confident in who God made you to be. You're not too short. You're not too tall. You're the right size. You have the right personality. You're the right nationality. You've been custom-made by the Creator of the universe. Put your shoulders back and hold your head high. You are not lacking. You haven't been shortchanged. You're not at a disadvantage. You have exactly what you need for where you are.

Get up every morning and remind yourself, "I have the strength, the talent, the friends, the resources, and the qualifications I need for today." If you'll do that, because your trust is in the Lord, I believe and declare you will never lack any good thing. God is going to take the small and turn it into much. He is going to multiply what you have and take you places you've never dreamed possible.

CHAPTER NINE

Keep Your Crown

When God breathed His life into you, He put a crown on your head. The psalmist called it "a crown of glory and honor." This crown represents your authority. It represents God's blessing and favor on your life. It's a reminder that you're not average, you're not mediocre: You are royalty. When you're wearing your crown, you'll have a sense of entitlement, thinking, *I have a right to be blessed. I have a right to live in victory. I have a right to overcome these challenges—not because I'm so great, so strong, or so talented, but because I'm wearing a crown of honor put there by my Creator.*

Your perception of yourself will determine what kind of life you live. If you think of yourself as being average, if you feel less-than because of what somebody said about you, if you live with guilt and condemnation because of past mistakes, that's going to limit your potential. What's happening? You're not wearing your crown.

Jesus said in the book of Revelation, "Hold fast to what you have so that no one will take your crown." Throughout life, there will always be someone or something trying to take your crown. People will talk about you, trying to make you look bad, to push you down. What they're really doing is trying to get your crown. Do yourself a favor. Don't let them have it. Eleanor Roosevelt said, "No one can make you feel inferior without your permission." Nobody can take your crown. You have to let go of what was said or done to you rather than let go of your crown.

> *Your perception of yourself will determine what kind of life you live.*

Somebody may say to you, "You're not that talented. You'll never be successful. You can't start your own business." Too often we think, *Yes, you're right. I don't really have what it takes. Look how long it's been. I'm not as smart as my cousin.* What's happening? You're letting go of your crown.

When those thoughts tell you that you're not attractive enough, just think a better thought and say, "No, thanks. You're not taking my crown. I know I am fearfully and wonderfully made. I know I am one of a kind." *You'll never get out of debt. You'll never send your children to college.* "No, thanks. I will lend and not borrow. Whatever I touch will prosper and succeed." You're not just being positive, you're holding on to your crown. Thoughts say, *Look at where you are in life. You should be ashamed of yourself. Look at the mistakes you've made. How many times have you failed?* "No, you're not having my crown. I may have fallen, but look at me now. I didn't stay down. I got back up again. I made mistakes, but that didn't change my name. I'm still a child of the Most High God." If you're going to keep your crown, you have to dig your heels in and say, "I'm not going to let what somebody said, or the fact that someone walked away, or that something didn't work out steal my sense of value. I know I have been crowned with honor."

The Crown of Honor Is Yours

When somebody tries to make you feel small, they make derogatory statements. Instead of being upset and believing what they say, just reach up and straighten your crown. They can't change who you are unless you allow them to. They don't control your destiny. They don't determine your value. They didn't breathe life into you; God did. He calls you a masterpiece. He says you're a king, a queen. You're supposed to reign in life. That's why He put the crown of honor on your head. It's to remind you of who you are.

The mistake we make too often is to believe the lies. Somebody says, "You're not that talented." Instead of saying, "No, thanks," we say, "Oh, you're right. Let me take off my crown. I thought I was talented." The message comes to us: "You're not royalty. You come from the wrong family. You'll never do anything great." Instead of ignoring it, not giving it the time of day, we think, *What was I thinking? Let me take off my crown.*

The enemy's main tool is deception. There's nothing he would love more than for you to go through life not wearing your crown, letting people and circumstances convince you that "You don't deserve to be blessed. You don't have what it takes. You've been through too much. You can't feel good about yourself." Don't you dare give away your crown! It belongs to you. It was put there by your Creator. It has nothing to do with how you feel, how you look, or what other people say. It's based solely on the fact that you are a child of the Almighty God. He has crowned you with glory and honor.

> *The enemy's main tool is deception.*

I know a young man who loved to play baseball. It was his passion growing up, but when he tried out for the school team, the coach didn't give him any chance. He said, "I'm sorry, son. You can't try out. You're too small. You could never make this team." The coach wasn't trying to be rude. He was just looking at it in the natural. But just because somebody doesn't believe in you doesn't mean that has to stop your dream.

The reason people don't always encourage you and cheer you on is because they can't feel what you feel. God didn't put the dream in them; He put the dream in you. Don't let their discouragement steal your enthusiasm. Keep your crown on. Keep believing. Keep hoping. Keep pursuing. You don't need everyone to be for you. You and God are a majority. When you're wearing your crown, God will open doors that no man can shut. He'll help you accomplish what you could not accomplish on your own. He wouldn't have put the dream in you if He didn't already have a way to bring it to pass.

This young man went home from school that day very discouraged; his heart was set on playing baseball. But instead of sitting around defeated, thinking he wasn't good enough, he kept his crown on. His attitude was, *The coach may say I'm too small, but I know I'm not a mistake. I'm the right size. I have what I need to fulfill my destiny.* A couple weeks later, the school announced that because so many boys had tried out for the baseball team, they were forming a second team. He tried out and made that team. He was excited about playing, even though he knew he was on the "lesser talented" team. Those two teams from the same school played in the same division with ten other teams. They ended up playing each other for the championship. This young man was the pitcher on the "lesser talented" team. Although he had been told he was too small, he struck out batter after batter after batter. They went on to beat the "more talented" team and won the division championship.

What am I saying? People don't determine your destiny. They don't know what's in you. Don't take off your crown because somebody judged you by what they saw on the outside. Somebody told you that you're not talented enough, not attractive enough, not tall enough, not smart enough. You don't have to have them cheering you on. Keep your crown on, keep being your best, keep honoring God, and He will get you to where you're supposed to be.

Approval Seekers

Jesus said to His critics, "Your approval or disapproval means nothing to Me." That's a powerful way to live. He was saying, "I know who I am, and nothing you do or don't do is going to change it. You can celebrate Me or you can crucify Me, but I'm keeping My crown." People are impulsive. One moment they can be cheering for you, and another moment they can be putting you down, trying to make you look bad. One moment Jesus was riding a donkey into Jerusalem and the people were waving palm branches, celebrating His arrival as though He was a king. A few days later, those same people were hollering, "Crucify Him! He doesn't deserve to live!"

If you base wearing your crown on whether or not people like you, whether or not they believe in you, you're going to be taking your crown off and then putting it back on throughout your whole life. You don't need other people's approval; you have Almighty God's approval. Our attitude should be, *You can be for me or against me, you can celebrate me or criticize me, but one thing is for certain: I'm not giving you my crown. I know who I am. I am royalty. I am accepted. I am approved. I am valuable.*

In the Scripture, Isaac said to his son Esau, "Your brother has carried away your blessing." Sometimes we let other people carry

---
You don't need other people's approval.

---

away our blessing. We let what they say about us—their disapproval and discouraging words—keep us from who we were meant to be. You have to put your foot down and say, "I'm not going to let people talk me out of my dreams. I'm not going to let a coworker make me feel inferior, as though I'm not good enough. I'm not going to let a coach, a teacher, or counselor talk me into living an average, mediocre, get-by life." You have seeds of greatness. You are destined to leave your mark on this generation. Don't let anyone carry away your blessing.

Where the Negative Thoughts Come From

When we look back, we can see that the enemy's been trying to get our crown from the beginning of time. In the Garden of Eden, Adam and Eve were living confident and secure. They were at peace with God, at peace with themselves. They were wearing their crowns. They knew they had God's blessing and favor. But one day the enemy deceived them into eating the forbidden fruit. When they did, immediately they were afraid. They ran and hid. In effect, they gave the enemy their crowns.

That's what happens when we surrender our crown of honor. It opens the door to fear, insecurity, and shame. We focus on what we're not, on the mistakes we've made, on what other people have said about us. Where there's no crown, there's no covering. There's no reminder of who we are. We believe those lies that can push us down.

When God came looking for Adam and Eve, He couldn't find them. He called out to Adam, "Where are you?" Adam said, "We're hiding because we're naked." God asked, "Who told you that you were naked?" God knew Adam had taken off his crown. God is asking us today, "Who told you there's something wrong with you? Who told you you're just average? That you can't accomplish your dreams? That you're too small? That you come from the wrong family? That you're not good enough?" I can assure you those negative thoughts didn't come from our God. You need to put your crown back on. You may have let some person or some event take it. The good news is that you can get it back. It's not too late; you have control over your crown.

It starts in your thinking. No more "I'm just a C student. I'm just average." Say, "I am an A student. I am full of wisdom. I will excel in school." When you think better, you live better. No more "I've been through too much. I lost a loved one. I'll never be happy again." Say, "God is giving me beauty for these ashes. What He started in my life, He will finish." Don't sit around feeling sorry for yourself. Put your crown back on. No more "I come from the wrong family. There's nothing special about me." Say, "I've been made in the image of Almighty God. I'm a masterpiece, one of a kind. I am a prized possession."

"Well, Joel, I could never do anything great in life. All the odds are against me." No, put your crown on and say, "I have the favor of God. I am equipped, empowered, and anointed." If you're going to reach your highest potential, you have to keep your crown on. It doesn't happen automatically. That's why the Scripture says to hold fast to what you have so that no one takes it away. Have you allowed something or someone to take your crown? Has a disappointment, a bad break, or a divorce caused you to lose your passion for life? Your crown is waiting for you. Have you let a mistake, a failure, or a bankruptcy convince you to settle for second best? You need to take

> *Hold fast to what you have so that no one takes it away.*

back your crown. You wouldn't be alive unless God had another victory in front of you. Start dreaming again. Start believing again. Start hoping again.

The Crown Gives You Favor

I talked to a young lady in the church lobby recently. She was very discouraged because her marriage didn't make it. Her husband left her for someone else. She was a beautiful woman, but now she was convinced that she wasn't attractive enough, talented enough, or smart enough. She had given her crown away. She told me all the things she should have done better. "If I'd only done this, if I'd only done that." In her mind, it was all her fault. But when somebody leaves your life, it doesn't necessarily mean there's something wrong with you. It could be the other person is the problem. Have you ever thought that perhaps they have some issues? If they left you, they'll leave the next person. But the accuser will work overtime trying to convince you that you don't measure up, that you're not valuable, and that there's nothing good in your future. He's trying to take your crown.

The Scripture says God will never leave us or forsake us. If they left you and you needed them, that would mean God was forsaking you. So you can conclude that if they left, you didn't need them. If they walked away, they weren't a part of your destiny. Isaiah said God will give you double for the unfair things that have happened. You may not realize it, but when they left, in a sense, they did you a favor. They set you up for what God really wants to do. He has somebody amazing in your future! A divine connection. Somebody better than you could imagine. Somebody who will treat you like the king, the queen, you were meant to be. But you have to do your part and put your crown back on. It's not going to happen if you go around negative, discouraged, and feeling unattractive. If you feel unattractive on the inside, you'll be unattractive on the outside. You carry yourself the way you feel about yourself.

I've seen ladies who don't have a lot of natural beauty, but on the inside they have it goin' on. When you're wearing your crown, you are confident and secure. You know you're a masterpiece, one of a kind, a prized possession. You're not dwelling on all the negative chatter—what you're not, what you don't have, or what other people are saying. You go through the day with a smile on your face, a spring in your step. You know you're royalty, that you've been crowned with glory and honor. When you think this way, you will live this way, and you're going to come into divine connections. You won't have to go after them. God will cause the right people to track you down.

Maybe you've been through a disappointment, a loss, something didn't work out. It would be easy for you to feel unattractive, not valuable, not excited about life. Put your crown back on. That crown is what gives you the favor. The

> *Don't let a disappointment or a loss carry away your blessing.*

crown is what causes you to stand out. Nothing that's happened has lessened your value.

You are still the prized possession, the apple of God's eye. Don't let a disappointment or a loss carry away your blessing. It's not the end. It's a new beginning.

Payback Is Coming

This is what a lady in the Scripture named Naomi had to do. She first lost her husband, then both her married sons died as well. Naomi was so discouraged she didn't think she could go on. She took off her crown. She had been a happy woman, full of joy and sweetness, fun to be around. Now she was bitter. She thought, *I'm done. I'll never be happy again.* She even changed her name from Naomi, which means "my joy," to Mara, which means "bitter." When people called her Naomi, she was so heartbroken she would say, "Please don't call me that. I'm too depressed. Call me Mara." She was saying, "Call me bitter." The problem is that when you take off your crown, you take off the favor, the honor, and the glory. That's what you need for God to pay you back. In those tough times, more than ever, you need to keep reminding yourself, "I am a child of the Most High God. I am extremely valuable. God has beauty for these ashes; double is coming my way."

Naomi thought her life was finished. She moved back to her hometown, planning on fading into the sunset. But when she saw some old friends and tried to persuade them to call her Mara, they said, "Naomi, what are you talking about? That's not who you are. You're not bitter. We're calling you, 'My joy.'" They kept calling her Naomi. Every time they did, they were prophesying her future. She was trying to stay in defeat, but they said, "No, you're coming into victory." She kept taking her crown off, and they kept putting it back on.

What am I saying? You need people around you who will remind you about who you are. Not people who will get bitter with you and agree with the defeat and mediocrity.

Stay close to people who will call you blessed, call you victorious, call you royalty. You want people in your life who will remind you that your best days are yet to come, that what was meant for your harm, God will use to your advantage—people who will help you keep your crown on. That's why every week I tell my listeners, "You are blessed, prosperous, redeemed, forgiven, talented, confident, strong, valuable—a masterpiece." What am I doing? Making sure that they're wearing their crown. Life tries to take it off them; my goal is to help people keep it on.

When Naomi went back to her hometown, her widowed daughter-in-law Ruth came with her. Ruth met a man named Boaz, and they married. One day they had a little baby boy. At this time, Naomi was way up there in years, and it didn't seem as though she had any reason to live. But when she saw that little baby, something came alive on the inside. The Scripture says, "The women in the town rejoiced, saying, 'Naomi, God has given you a son. This baby will restore your youth.'"

She felt a new sense of purpose. She took care of that little baby as though he were her own. Naomi thought she'd never be happy again, but now she was more fulfilled than ever. That was God paying her back for the unfair things that had happened—she had her crown back on.

Are you wearing your crown today? Or have you let a disappointment, a loss, or a bad break convince you to take it off? Nothing that's happened to you has stopped God's plan.

> *Nothing that's happened to you has stopped God's plan.*

He knows how to give beauty for ashes, how to turn mourning into dancing. As Naomi did, you may have taken your crown off, thinking that you've seen your best days, but you need to get ready. The latter part of your life is going to be better than the former part. God still has a purpose for you to fulfill. He still has something amazing in your future. Put your crown back on.

Rediscover Who You Really Are

I heard a version of the mythological story about Helen of Troy. She was an extremely beautiful queen, a young woman born into royalty, loved and admired by all the people. But one day she was kidnapped and taken away to a foreign country. With all the confusion, she was stricken with amnesia. She couldn't remember her name or where she was from. She ended up living on the streets, homeless, being taken advantage of. Although she had royalty in her blood and was a respected and admired queen in her hometown, nobody knew where she was and she didn't know who she was. Back at home, her friends and family never gave up on her. Even though years and years had passed, they believed she was still alive. Then one man who loved her dearly, who had taken care of her when she was growing up, set out to try to find her.

While he was searching the streets of a faraway country, he saw this pitiful-looking woman who was sitting by the water. Her clothes were ragged, her hair was matted, and her face was battered and bruised. He was about to pass by, but something about her looked strangely familiar to him. The man asked her what her name was. She mumbled something and wouldn't really talk. He looked closer and became even more intrigued. He asked if he could see her hands. He remembered the line prints on Helen's hands. When the woman showed him her hands, he was astonished. He couldn't believe it. He whispered, "Helen." She looked at him, confused. He said, "You are Helen of Troy. You are the queen. Helen, don't you remember?" Suddenly it was as though a light turned on, and her face brightened. The fog lifted. She rediscovered who she really was and hugged her friend. They traveled back to her hometown, and once again she became the queen she was meant to be.

Similar to Helen, too many people today

are suffering from spiritual amnesia. They were born into royalty, created to reign in life. God crowned them with honor and glory, but they've somehow forgotten who they are. Because of bad breaks, disappointments, and the mistakes they've made, they feel beaten down by life and are living far below their privileges, thinking that they're average. As this man did for Helen, I'm here to remind you of whose you are. You are a child of the Most High God. You have royal blood flowing through your veins. There is a crown of honor that belongs to you. Your mind may be in a fog, but I believe that in your spirit something is coming alive. Strongholds that have held you back are being broken. The chains of defeated thinking and a negative mentality are being loosed. You're going to rediscover who you really are. You are not average or mediocre; you are royalty—a king, a queen. Now do your part and put your crown back on.

I read about an eight-year-old boy who was born a few years before the French Revolution.

His father was King Louis XVI. During all the violent insurrection, first his entire family was imprisoned, and then both his mother and father were condemned to death. In January 1793, his father was brought out to the public square and beheaded, and his mother suffered the same fate the following October. The young prince remained a threat to the leaders of the revolution, who determined to "retrain" Louis XVII to make him compliant to the revolution and to accuse his mother of wrongdoing. Stories circulated that the royal heir to the throne was subjected to extreme cruelty, and attempts were made to teach him to say profane things, to lie, to cheat, and to do wrong. While no one knows exactly what happened, in my imagination I can see him putting his foot down when they tried to make him speak in profanities and saying, "No, I'm not going to do it. I was born to be a king. I will not talk that way." When they tried to get him to lie, to cheat, to compromise, the same thing: "I am a king. I will not do it."

When the enemy tries to reprogram your thinking, telling you that you're average, you're ordinary, just say, "No, thanks. I'm a king. I will not think that way." When thoughts try to convince you to live a mediocre, defeated life, say, "No, thanks. I know I am royalty. I will not live beneath my privileges. I know I am a child of the Most High God."

I'm asking you to keep your crown on. You may have been through disappointments and loss. Life will try to take it. You have to hold fast to what God has given you. Don't let anyone or anything carry away your blessing. If you'll make this decision with me that you're going to keep your crown on, I believe and declare you will reign in life, rise higher, accomplish your dreams, and reach the fullness of your destiny.

CHAPTER TEN

Just Remember

When you look back over your life, consider some of the things you've faced that at the time you didn't think you could make it through. The obstacle was so large, the breakup hurt you so badly, the medical report was so negative. You didn't see a way, but God turned it around. He gave you strength when you didn't think you could go on. He brought the right person when you thought you'd always be lonely. He promoted you, gave you that good break, and things fell into place. Now you're further along than you ever imagined.

That wasn't a lucky break. It wasn't a

coincidence. It was the hand of God. You should have been stuck, addicted, broke, depressed, and lonely, but God made a way when you didn't see a way. You can say what I say: "I didn't get to where I am by myself. It wasn't just my good luck, my hard work, or my talent. It was the favor of God. He made things happen that I could never make happen on my own."

But none of us like difficulties. If we had a choice, we wouldn't go through them. However, those challenges not only prepared you for your future, now you have a history with God. When you're in a tough time, and you don't see a way out, instead of being discouraged and negative, you can go back and remember how God turned your health around. Remember how He gave you that baby when the specialist said you couldn't have a child. Remember how He brought you out of that trouble that you got yourself in.

When you remember how God has protected you, promoted you, healed you, and restored you, faith will rise in your heart.

Instead of thinking, *I'll never get out of this problem*, you'll say with confidence, "God did it for me once; He'll do it for me again. He made

When you come through a challenge, that victory will be the fuel you use that gets you to the next level.

a way in the past; I know He's going to make a way in the future." Don't complain about the problem. It's not random. You're going to need that victory in the future. God is taking you from glory to glory. When you come through this challenge, that victory will be the fuel you use that gets you to the next level of glory.

Develop the Habit of Remembering

This is what happened with the Israelites. They were up against huge armies, against nations that were stronger, had more equipment, and were more skilled in warfare. The Israelites had just come out of slavery. They had no military training or weapons; they were just trying to survive in the desert. They were headed toward the Promised Land, but they had one enemy after another to overcome. They were very discouraged. They didn't know how they could do it.

God said to them in Deuteronomy 7, "You may think, 'How can we conquer these nations that are much stronger than us?' But don't be afraid. Just remember what God did to Pharaoh. You saw with your own eyes the miraculous signs and the amazing power God used to bring you out." God was saying, "When it looks impossible, when you don't see a way out, the way to stay encouraged and keep your hopes up is to remember what God has done."

As was true for the Israelites, we have seen with our own eyes those times when God made a way. You thought you were stuck, but God opened a door. He caused somebody to be good to you. You faced the loss of a loved one, and you thought you would never be happy again, but God lifted you out of that pit. He turned your mourning into dancing.

When you face tough times and your dream looks impossible, every voice says, "It's never going to happen." Just remember. Go back and replay your victories. Relive the times God made a way. Remember how He put you at the right place at the right time and you met that person and fell in love. Remember how He spared your life from that accident. Remember how the medical report said you shouldn't be here, but you are alive, strong, and healthy today.

If you're going to overcome obstacles, if you're going to reach your highest potential, you have to learn to remember. When you're constantly thinking about God's goodness, how He's protected you, vindicated you, and promoted you, not only will faith rise in your heart, but it's that attitude of expectancy that allows God to do great things. On a regular basis, we should go back over the major victories in our life. Remember the day your child was born. That was a great miracle. Remember how God gave you that job, how He protected you, and how you met the right person. Develop this habit of remembering what God has done. These are the better thoughts that will propel you forward in the future.

I remember in my early twenties when I walked into a jewelry store to buy a battery for my watch. I was simply minding my own business when out walked the most beautiful girl I'd ever seen. It was Victoria. We ended up dating for a year and a half, and she couldn't keep her hands off me, so we got married. At least that's the way I remember it! I recognize that encounter wasn't a coincidence. That wasn't a lucky break. That was God directing my steps, putting me at the right place at the right time, and He used a battery to do it. When I think about that, it reminds me how God is in control of my life. If He was directing my steps back then, I know He's directing my steps right now.

The Mercies of God

When the apostle Paul talks about "the mercies of God" in the Scripture, he doesn't use the singular but the plural. Every one of us has experienced some of these mercies. For me, walking into the jewelry store that day was one of the many mercies of God.

When I was first married, I was driving on the freeway during a big rainstorm and lost control of my car. I started spinning around and around, crossing the different lanes of the freeway. At one point I looked up and saw this eighteen-wheeler coming right at me. At that moment, I was going in the wrong direction. We were so close I felt as though I could touch his front grille, and I thought, *That's it. I'm done.* All I could say was "Jesus." When you're in that kind of trouble, you don't have to pray long. Somehow that big truck missed me, and the driver pulled his big rig over. He got out of his cab, walked over to my car, and when he looked into my window at me, his eyes were very big. He said, "I can't believe I didn't run over you, but at the last second a big gust of wind blew my truck into the other lane." He said it was the wind; I know it was the mercies of God.

When our son, Jonathan, was less than a year old, we were on a boat with some friends. He was in the baby carrier, and we'd set it on the bench in the boat. As we were traveling along, something whispered to Victoria, "Go hold on to your son." She walked over and held on to the baby carrier. About thirty seconds later, the boat hit a huge wave and everything that wasn't tied down went flying overboard. Jonathan would have been thrown into the water if not for the mercies of God.

He said it was the wind; I know it was the mercies of God.

Many of you can join me in saying that you wouldn't be alive if it wasn't for God's mercies. Some of the things you've done—

the crowds you used to run with, the drugs, the alcohol, the reckless driving, the freak accidents—should have taken you out. But God showed you some of His mercies—not once, but again and again.

Maybe you shouldn't have the position you're in at your workplace. You weren't the most qualified, but the mercies of God gave it to you. Or perhaps that sickness said it was going to be the end, but the mercies of God said, "This is not your time." When you recognize what God has done, that all through your life it's been His hand getting you to where you are, then it's easy to honor God; it's easy to be grateful. It's easy to serve, to give, and to help others. You realize that where you are in life is because of the mercies of God.

You know you're driving a mercy car. You're living in a mercy house. You're working at a mercy job. You didn't just marry over your head, you married mercy. Maybe you felt you were about to have a nervous breakdown, but mercy showed up. You should be depressed, but mercy turned you around. You could be in prison, but mercy kept you out. Perhaps you even tried to take your own life, but mercy kept you alive. Mercy gave you that baby. Mercy gave you that idea. Mercy opened that door. Don't take it for granted. Keep it in the forefront of your mind.

You're not just lucky; you don't just keep beating the odds. It's the mercies of God. In fact, the reason you're still here, the reason that truck couldn't run over you, the reason those drugs couldn't kill you, the reason the sickness couldn't take you out is because God has a destiny for you to fulfill. He has an assignment for you to accomplish. His mercies are never going to give up on you. His calling is irrevocable. He chose you before you could choose Him. You might as well recognize you're a marked man, a marked woman. The Creator of the universe has His hand on your life. The

You're not just lucky. You might as well recognize you're a marked man, a marked woman.

sooner you surrender your will to His, the better off you're going to be. You're not giving up anything. You're gaining purpose, your destiny, a life that He's designed, a life more rewarding than you ever imagined. You love Him because He first loved you.

The Goodness of God

David said, "If it had not been for the goodness of God, where would I be?" He was saying in effect, "If God had not shown me some of His mercies, I wouldn't have defeated Goliath. Without the mercies of God, I wouldn't have been able to outlast King Saul when he was trying to kill me in the desert. I wouldn't have been restored after my mistake with Bathsheba without God's mercy."

A young man told me how he's had a serious drug problem for many years. One day he was partying with some friends and accidentally got several different types of drugs mixed up. He took so many that his friends began to panic. They thought for sure he would pass out or have convulsions. But those drugs had no effect on him. It was as though they had lost all their power. He said, "Joel, I came to church today because I'm one lucky guy." I told him what I'm telling you. It's a lot more than luck; it's the mercies of God.

Psalm 129 says, "From my earliest youth my enemies have persecuted me, but they have never been able to finish me off." Sometimes you need to just thank God that you're still here. Cancer couldn't finish you off. Depression couldn't finish you off. That divorce, the legal problems, the bankruptcy couldn't finish you off. Perhaps it was the person talking about you who couldn't finish you off. The haters, the critics, and the naysayers tried to push you down, doing their best to make you look bad, but their best was not powerful enough. You're still standing, you're still strong, you still have a smile. They couldn't finish you off. You got knocked down, but you got back up again. You had a setback or a breakup, but you're still in the game. You went through a loss, but you didn't get bitter, you kept moving forward. That setback could not finish you off.

When my father was a little boy, he fell into a large fire. That fire should have taken his life, but the fire could not finish him off. He was raised during the Great Depression with next to nothing, but poverty could not finish him off. His first marriage as a young man didn't make it. He was told he could never be in ministry after that, but divorce couldn't finish him off. Years later, some people turned on him and asked him to leave his church, but betrayal couldn't finish him off. He had high blood pressure most of his life, but that couldn't finish him off. He had to raise my brother, Paul, and that came very, very close!

What am I saying? God has the final say. People can't finish you off. A bad break, betrayal, rejection, or sickness can't do it. When the enemy comes in like a flood, the

Scripture says God raises up a barrier. God will put a stop to it. The forces that are for you are greater than the forces that are against you.

What You Don't Even Know About

You may be in a difficult time. Don't get discouraged. Just remember the Red Seas that God has already parted in your life. Remember how God delivered you from the Pharaoh, so to speak. He snatched you out of a harmful situation. He closed that door that would have proven a big mistake. He blessed you with that position you didn't seem to deserve. You have a history with God. You've seen His mercies—not once, but again and again—showing out in your life.

You need to announce to that cancer, "You can't finish me off. The God who spoke worlds into existence breathed His life into me. He controls the number of my days." Announce to that depression, fear, and anxiety, "You're not going to finish me off. God promised I will finish my course with joy." Don't get discouraged because of that person in the office who's trying to push you down and make you look bad. They don't control your destiny. They can't stop God's plan for your life. When those negative thoughts come telling you, *This sickness is going to sink you. This legal problem is going to be the end,* just answer back, "You don't realize who you're dealing with. I'm a child of the Most High God. You cannot finish me off."

God is called the author and the finisher of our faith. What He started in your life, He will finish—not a bad break, not a disappointment, not a sickness. God is the finisher. In the New Testament days, Saul was one of the greatest enemies of the church. He was headed toward Damascus to persecute believers. He had permission from the courts to arrest any followers of Christ. This man was on a mission with his papers in hand. The believers in Damascus had this powerful enemy coming straight toward them and they didn't even know it. He was going to cause them tremendous heartache and pain. It looked inevitable. But suddenly a bright light shone down on Saul from Heaven. The light was so strong it knocked him off his horse. He fell flat on his back and couldn't see. In a split second, God stopped the persecutor in his tracks…and in the process changed him into an apostle.

We all need to realize there were times in our past when we knew nothing about it, but something was coming our way—a bad break, an accident, a sickness. It was already en route with papers in hand. It should have finished us off, but God said, "No, I don't think so. That's My son, that's My daughter. I'm putting a stop to it." That eighteen-wheeler should've finished me off, but God pushed the truck out of the way. There have been many things you knew nothing about, but God stopped a cancer, stopped a betrayal, or stopped

You have no idea of all that is going on behind the scenes.

a rejection. It was all behind the scenes. That's the mercies of God. Sometimes you need to thank God for what didn't happen. Thank Him for the enemies He stopped that you know nothing about.

Remember the Right Things

"Joel, this sounds encouraging, but I've had a lot of bad breaks and gone through a lot of disappointments. I didn't get the promotion for which I worked so hard. This person walked out of my life." Here's the problem: You're remembering the wrong things. I can't find one place in the Scripture where we're told to remember our defeats, remember our failures, or remember our bad breaks. "Well, my company laid me off twenty-seven years ago. It wasn't right." May I tell you this respectfully? It's time to get over it. Quit thinking about it, quit talking about it, and quit reliving it. All that it's doing is depressing you. You're making yourself defeated. Has

God done anything good for you in the last twenty-seven years? Have you seen one promotion, one healing, one sign of His favor?

Start remembering your victories, the times God healed you, the times He promoted you, the times He stopped the accidents, the times He turned the problems around. When you're remembering the right things, you're going to move forward in faith. You'll see more of God's favor.

David said in Psalm 34, "Let all who are discouraged take heart." He goes on to tell us how to do it. The next verse says, "Come, let's talk about God's goodness. I prayed and the Lord answered my prayer." He was saying, "When you're discouraged, when you don't see a way out, come and let's talk—not about your problems, not about what didn't work out. No, let's talk about God's greatness. Let's talk about your answered prayers. Let's talk about the Red Seas that have been parted."

What you're saying in your tough times will make or break you. If you go around saying, "I'll never get out of this problem.

It's just too big," you'll get stuck. Turn it around and say, "God, I want

> *Remember the Red Seas that have been parted.*

to thank You for Your greatness in my life. Thank You for giving me this job. Lord, thank You for freeing me from this addiction." When you're always talking about God's goodness, you won't be down and discouraged. You'll have a spring in your step, a smile on your face. You'll know that God has done it for you in the past, and He'll do it for you again in the future.

Mountable

A friend of mine is a big-time fisherman. In his house, he has several impressive mounted fish on the walls. There's a large swordfish over his fireplace, and a gorgeous blue marlin hanging on the wall next to his television. In his family room, there's a huge hammerhead shark, perhaps ten feet long, on the wall. The first time I went into his house, we spent over an hour just going from room to room, taking in all his trophy fish. He described where he caught them, how he caught them, and what kind of bait he used. That blue marlin fought him for over two hours before he reeled it in. What's interesting is that over the years he's caught a lot of small fish—trout, flounder, and sea bass—but none of them are up on the walls. He mounted only the large fish. The small ones were fine, had value, and could be eaten, but they weren't worthy of being mounted.

In the same way, God has done many great things for us. He provides our daily needs and gives us strength, wisdom, and protection. We're all thankful. We're grateful for His goodness. But God wants to do some things in your life that are mountable, some things that are so big, so impressive, you will want to hang them on your wall, in a manner of speaking. When people come over, when they see you, you have something to point at. "This is what God did in my life." Do you know what our facility, the former Compaq Center, is? It's mountable. People driving on the freeway point it out and say, "That used to be a sports arena, but now it's Lakewood Church." They're saying, "Look at what God has done."

My mother was diagnosed with terminal cancer and given a few weeks to live. Today, thirty-five years later, she's still alive, healthy and strong. Everywhere she goes she has something to talk about, something impressive, something out of the ordinary, a trophy of God's goodness. You can look back and see times when God did something unusual in your life. Maybe you shouldn't be living in the house that you're in now. You didn't have the funds, but things fell into place. You know it was the hand of God. That's mountable.

Perhaps you struggled with an addiction. You were off course, but today you're healthy, you're clean, you're free, you're being a blessing to others. As is true of my mother, you are a living testimony. You don't have to go look for a miracle; you are a miracle. When you need to be encouraged, just go look at yourself in the mirror. You shouldn't be where you are. Perhaps you should still be struggling, addicted, angry, depressed, and lonely, but God in His mercy showed up and said, "I don't think so." When it looked impossible, He stopped it. He's given you something to talk about. You're a trophy of God's goodness. Now here's the key: Don't let what once was a miracle become ordinary. Don't lose the awe of what God has done.

Be like my friend. When I went to his house, he couldn't wait to show off all the impressive fish he had caught. Everywhere you go, talk about God's goodness—not bragging about yourself, but bragging about what God has done. I must have heard my father tell the story a thousand times of how he gave his life to Christ. It happened when he was seventeen, but at seventy-five years old he was still telling

> *You don't have to go look for a miracle; you are a miracle.*

it as though it happened just yesterday. He never lost the amazement. When you constantly think about what God has done, when you relive your miracles, when you're always in awe of His goodness, you are putting yourself in position for God to do something even more amazing. God wants to give you some new things to mount. Get ready for favor that you haven't yet seen, for opportunity, influence, and promotion. He has something out of the ordinary, something impressive, a new level coming your way.

Consider Your History

On one occasion, the disciples were in a boat. Just a few hours before, they had seen Jesus take five loaves of bread and two fish, pray over them, and feed some fifteen thousand people. At the end of that day, He told the disciples to gather up the leftovers, get in the boat, and cross to the other side of the lake. Now it was the middle of the night. Strong winds suddenly swept down on the lake, and the waves were very high. The disciples were concerned for their safety, when they saw Jesus walking on the water. At first, in the pitch black of night, they thought He was a ghost. They finally recognized Him and invited Him into their boat. When He got into the boat, the winds and waves calmed down immediately. They were relieved they were okay.

But the Scripture gives us insight into why they were so worried. It says, "They didn't consider the miracle of the loaves." They were so stressed out by the nighttime storm and high waves, they forgot how earlier that day they had seen with their own eyes one of the greatest miracles ever recorded. If they had just remembered what God had done, if they had just remembered the miracle, they would have stayed in faith. They would have been calm, knowing that everything would be okay despite the waves. What's interesting is that they were out on the lake because they had been obedient. They had done what

Jesus asked. They were faithful. Where they missed it was their not remembering what God had done.

Are you doing what they did? Are you letting your circumstances, a medical report, or a financial situation cause you to live worried, stressed out? Why don't you start considering your miracles? Look back over your life. Remember the time God showed up and suddenly turned it around. Look on your walls and relive some of those mountable things God has done.

How are you going to defeat the Pharaohs in your life? How are you going to overcome those large obstacles? God

Why don't you start considering your miracles?

is saying to you what He said to the Israelites: Just remember. You have a history with God. Every victory He's given you wasn't just for that time; it was so you could go back and use that as fuel to build your faith. If you are low on faith, you need to go back and get some fuel. It's in your past victories.

Don't talk about your problems; talk about the greatness of God.

Remember, the enemy cannot finish you off; God has the final say. If you'll develop this habit of just remembering, I believe and declare that God is about to show out in your life. As you think better, you're going to live better. He's going to give you something new to mount. You're going to rise higher, accomplish your dreams, go places you never thought possible.

ACKNOWLEDGMENTS

In this book I offer many stories shared with me by friends, members of our congregation, and people I've met around the world. I appreciate and acknowledge their contributions and support. Some of those mentioned in the book are people I have not met personally, and in a few cases, we've changed the names to protect the privacy of individuals. I give honor to all those to whom honor is due. As the son of a church leader and a pastor myself, I've listened to countless sermons and presentations, so in some cases I can't remember the exact source of a story.

I am indebted to the amazing staff of Lakewood Church, the wonderful members of Lakewood who share their stories with

me, and those around the world who gen-
erously support our ministry and make it
possible to bring hope to a world in need.
I am grateful to all of those who follow our
services on television, the Internet, SiriusXM,
and through the podcasts. You are all part
of our Lakewood family.

I offer special thanks also to all the pastors across the country who are members of
our Champions Network.

Once again, I am grateful for a wonderful team of professionals who helped me put
this book together for you. Leading them
is my Faith Words/Hachette publisher, Rolf
Zettersten, along with team members Patsy
Jones, Billy Clark, and Becky Hughes. I truly
appreciate the editorial contributions of word-
smith Lance Wubbels.

I am grateful also to my literary agents Jan
Miller Rich and Shannon Marven at Dupree
Miller & Associates.

And last but not least, thanks to my
wife, Victoria, and our children, Jonathan
and Alexandra, who are my sources of daily

inspiration, as well as our closest family members who serve as day-to-day leaders of our ministry, including my mother, Dodie; my brother, Paul, and his wife, Jennifer; my sister, Lisa, and her husband, Kevin; and my brother-in-law, Don, and his wife, Jackelyn.

We Want to Hear from You!

Each week, I close our international television broadcast by giving the audience an opportunity to make Jesus the Lord of their lives. I'd like to extend that same opportunity to you.

Are you at peace with God? A void exists in every person's heart that only God can fill. I'm not talking about joining a church or finding religion. I'm talking about finding life and peace and happiness. Would you pray with me today? Just say, "Lord Jesus, I repent of my sins. I ask You to come into my heart. I make You my Lord and Savior."

Friend, if you prayed that simple prayer, I believe you have been "born again." I encourage you to attend a good, Bible-based church and keep God in first place in your life.

For free information on how you can grow stronger in your spiritual life, please feel free to contact us.

Victoria and I love you, and we'll be praying for you. We're believing for God's best for you, that you will see your dreams come to pass. We'd love to hear from you!

To contact us, write to:

Joel and Victoria Osteen
P.O. Box 4600
Houston, TX 77210

Or you can reach us online at www.joelosteen.com.

STAY**CONNECTED,**
BE**BLESSED.**

From thoughtful articles to powerful blogs,
podcasts and more, JoelOsteen.com is full of
inspirations that will give you encouragement and
confidence in your daily life.

AVAILABLE ON JOELOSTEEN.COM

This daily devotional from Joel
and Victoria will help you grow
in your relationship with the Lord
and equip you to be everything
God intends you to be.

 Joel Osteen
STREAMING

Miss a broadcast? Watch Joel
Osteen on demand, and see
Joel LIVE on Sundays.

 Joel Osteen
PODCAST

The podcast is a great way
to listen to Joel where you
want, when you want.

CONNECT WITH US

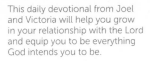

Join our
community of
believers on your
favorite social
network.

TAKE HOPE WITH YOU

Get the inspiration and
encouragement of Joel Osteen
on your iPhone, iPad or Android
device! Our app puts Joel's
messages, devotions and more
at your fingertips.

Thanks for helping us make a difference in
the lives of millions around the world.